THE ORACLE OF

COLOMBO

HOW ARTHUR C. CLARKE
REVEALED THE FUTURE

Author: Dr. Joseph N. Pelton

Editor: Peter Marshall

This book is published by the Arthur C. Clarke Foundation, a not-for-profit organization dedicated to the lifetime works and achievements of Arthur C. Clarke (www.clarkefoundation.org)

ISBN-13: 978-1502723512

REVIEWS

Arthur C. Clarke comes alive in Joe Pelton's narrative, as a man whose striking powers of imagination, scientific prescience and moral concern combined to provide humankind a lasting model of how to think about the future. While the scope of Clarke's concerns was vast his focus on the implications of technology for human society was singular. **- Amy Zalman, Ph.D., President, World Future Society.**

Arthur Clarke never patented the concept of satellite telecommunications which he dreamed-up, creating perhaps the largest open source communications project benefiting billions of people.. Joe Pelton has done a remarkable job telling the story of one of the world's foremost thinkers and writers. **- Michael Potter, Chairman and CEO of Paradigm Ventures**

Arthur Charles Clarke was in many ways the seminal mind of the 20th century. His awesome anticipation of satellites, computers, email and text messaging, artificial intelligence, e-commerce, driverless-cars, green energy and much more, stimulated most of the formidable innovations of the 21st century. Doubtless, there's more to come. The Oracle of Colombo: How Arthur C. Clarke Revealed the Future vividly shows us just how much we are indebted to Sir Arthur for the technological bounties we enjoy today. **- Tedson Meyers, Chairman, Arthur C. Clarke Foundation**

Dedication

This book is dedicated to all the people that have played a role in the creation and success of the Arthur C. Clarke Foundation since it was founded some three decades ago at the White House in 1983 as part of the World Communications Year ceremonies. This dedication includes all of the members of the Board of the Foundation and its chairmen, John L. McLucas (now deceased) and Tedson Meyers. It also includes the students that have received Arthur C. Clarke educational awards and fellowship recipients at the Huish College in the U.K., at the Challenger Center, at the International Space University, at the International Association for the Advancement of Space Safety, through the educational programs of the Universities Space Research Association and through the Solar Electric Light Foundation (SELF). This dedication also goes to our spin-offs, namely the Arthur C. Clarke Institute for Space Science Education as well as the newly formed Arthur C. Clarke Center for the Human Imagination at the University of California at San Diego. Further this dedication extends to the recipients of the Dr. Burton I. Edelson fellowships at George Washington University which the Foundation established, plus all the participants in Clarke Foundation sponsored symposia, workshops and award ceremonies that have been carried out over the years in the United States, in the United Kingdom, and in Sri Lanka. The total number of people who have served on the Board and Advisory Council, received awards, participated in educational programs and symposia and attended the awards programs now number in the many thousands. The purpose of the Arthur C. Clarke Foundation is to keep the memory and spirit of Sir Arthur Clarke alive, give awards in his name, but also to support education and innovation in the world as well. This book is yet another attempt to accomplish all these goals.

Joseph N. Pelton
Arlington, Virginia

Acknowledgements

A number of people were instrumental in the development of this project and the publishing of this book. There are a number of people who have contributed to the educational fund and these have included Frederick Ordway, Ed Horowitz, Burton Edelson, Delbert Smith, Joseph Pelton, Jeff Goldstein and Timothy Logue among others. Specific assistance was provided by Neil McAleer who encouraged the initial effort to catalogue many of Arthur C. Clarke's predictions and an assessment of which ones had been realized in his book *Visionary.* Finally and most particularly I would like to acknowledge the support of the Arthur C. Clarke Foundation Board and especially Peter Marshall who painstakingly edited this book, served as a fact checker, and worked with the publisher to bring this book to press. I have now collaborated with Peter Marshall in the writing and publishing of eight books and as always it has been a treat and a joy to work with him.

Joseph N. Pelton
Arlington, Virginia

Table of Contents

PART I:

Clarke's Predictions, Then and Now

Chapter 1

Arthur C. Clarke:

The 20th Century Leonardo

"If we could see the future--with absolute certainty--there would be no purpose in living. Nothing could change the inevitable; we would be robots, unable to deviate from a predetermined program."
Arthur C. Clarke "Greetings, Carbon-based Bi-Peds", St. Martin's Press, New York (1999)

"The Hazards of Prophecy? The Failure of Nerve and the Failure of Imagination"
Arthur C. Clarke, "Profiles of the Future", Guernsey Press, Great Britain (1988)

"Every revolutionary idea seems to evoke three stages of reaction. They may be summed up by the phrases: (1) It's completely impossible. (2) It's possible, but it's not worth doing. (3) I said it was a good idea all along".
"The Quotes of Arthur C. Clarke" - Clarke Institute for Space Science Education.

"As our own species is in the process of proving, one cannot have superior science and inferior morals. The combination is unstable and self-destroying."
"The Quotes of Arthur C. Clarke" - Clarke Institute for Space Science Education.

Arthur C. Clarke was the Leonardo da Vinci of the 20th Century. His inventions in communications, transport, navigation and tracking, his amazing literary and cinematic achievements, and his incredible predictions are truly a marvel. No one in recent times connected the synapses in the left and right lobes of their brains as did Sir Arthur.

He was at once an artist, an inventor, a scientist, a creator, a systems synthesizer, and a futurist *par excellence*. We who knew him, corresponded with him, admired him, and even created a Foundation in his honor, never really quite knew why he was so extraordinary. But we still feel it is very important to find out, because the future of humankind might perhaps hinge on finding the answer to this puzzle? We need to evolve as a race to be more Intelligent, more Innovative, more Imaginative and not be quite so Ignorant, Insensitive and Immoral. This "**Six I's**" formula is so very simple that we at least can hope to get it right eventually. The juxtaposition of the good three **I's** versus the bad three **I's** will, however, define a good deal of our future whether we are talking about war, climate change, gaps in education, health care or wealth, or moral choices involving the development of new technology.

Why was he able to create some of the world's most compelling science fiction literature, make extraordinary films, envision the geosynchronous communications satellite, help develop radar systems for automated takeoffs and landings, explore and write about the oceans in great depth (pun intended) and also find time to make some of the most compelling predictions of the 21st century—all within the constraints of a single brain? The Arthur C. Clarke Center for the Human Imagination at the University of California in San Diego (UCSD), among its many goals, seeks to answer that very question. In short, why are some unique individuals able to move across the axis of artistic creativity and imagination into the sphere of engineering and math and science and then back in the blink of the eye or the snap of a neuron? These extraordinarily adept polymaths seem to be the unique systems synthesizers who can think with the left and right side of their brain simultaneously.

The ultimate question posed by the life, accomplishments and visionary predictions of Sir Arthur Clarke comes down to this—Imagination and Insight Tempered with Morality. This book seeks to trace Arthur C. Clarke's lifelong odyssey into the future. The goal is to mine, dissect and interpret his brain and his marvelous insights. The mission is to probe and better understand his visionary imagination and insight that so often revealed a view of the future yet to be.

We often ask ourselves: What makes humanity different? Mynah birds can talk. Chimpanzees can make and use tools. Dolphins have clearly demonstrated communications skills and have a documented language. We are currently even teaching deaf dogs to use sign language. If the species *homo sapiens* have a unique claim to fame, it seems to come down to a very limited set of skills. Ray Kurzweil, author of *The Singularity is Near* and *How to Create a Mind* has said: "In human hands, our intelligence has enabled us to overcome the restriction of our biological heritage and to change ourselves in the process. We are the only species that does this." Thus it comes down to the fact that the most significant human attributes appear to be **'Imagination and Vision'** and Arthur C. Clarke had a brain that worked in overdrive in these domains.

Uniquely he was also able in many instances to go on beyond the vision and the imaginative insight and then do the math to show his ideas were feasible. Unlike many visionaries, he was finally able to engineer his ideas to make them a reality. Except Arthur also had yet another dimension represented by a moral compass. This compass always pointed toward world peace, racial and cultural harmony, universal education, recyclable green energy, and preservation of the world's biosphere.

How did Einstein have the ability to conceive of the space-time continuum? What leap of vision led him to conceive gravity as simply being the distortion to the spatial continuum made by mass? How was

Hubble able to conceive of entire galaxies of stars rushing away from the Milky Way and to imagine the universe to be much more vast than anyone ever had thought before? How were James Clerk Maxwell and Heinrich Hertz imaginative enough to understand for the first time that all forms of electrical and magnetic energy were in fact actually one and the same? How were Bach, Beethoven and Brahms able to compose such transcendental music? How were Michelangelo and Leonardo di Vinci able to conceive and execute their artistry with truly breakthrough vision? These are perhaps questions we will someday cogently explain.

Arthur's "Seven Wonders of the World"

There was a remarkable insight into the breadth of Arthur C. Clarke's mind in 1997 when he was one of the contributors to a BBC TV series asked to choose their "Seven Wonders of the World." A film crew went to his home in Sri Lanka and recorded his wide-ranging choices - here is his eclectic list, together with some of his comments:

Saturn V - "The most powerful machine ever built and flown by man ... equivalent of 150-million horsepower ... 300,000 people were involved ... it cost $20 billion ... and a page of history was turned."

Sigiriya - "The 5th century lion rock in Sri Lanka is as much a wonder of the world as the Pyramids or Angkor Wat ... but on a human scale .. its mystery has haunted me for years."

The microchip - An invention that is a million times faster and thousands of times cheaper than mechanical computers ... microchips are now running our world like electronic slaves."

The Mandebrot Set - "A paradox - was it man-made or something he discovered? It is a formula which produces the most beautiful images ....the only way I know of getting some idea of infinity."

Bach's Toccata and Fugue in D Minor - "It was played by my

11

schoolmaster at Huish when he tried to introduce us country bumpkins to music ... it is the most dramatic and awe-inspiring music ever written."

The Giant Squid - "I have always been fascinated by strange monsters ... this may be the largest of all animals, growing to 100-ft or more ... larger than anyone imagined .. a battle between a giant squid and a sperm whale is something to behold."

SS433 - "The universe is full of wonders but this astronomical object is unique. What is it? It has two beams or jets travelling at millions of miles an hour. Is it a natural object? ... Is it the product of technology from another civilization?   ... I don't know".

An Imagination So Vivid and Compelling

If we cannot definitely answer what is the basis of human intelligence and vision, we might at least try to unlock some part of the magic of Arthur C. Clarke's amazingly insightful predictions. The analysis that follows thus seeks to understand somewhat better how and when his predictions have come true and in some cases are still coming to fruition. This can be accomplished by probing his special skill to envision new technology, to anticipate in a systematic way the social, economic and philosophical implications of these new human capabilities, and to look into that future through the crystal of literary artistry and moral vision—often revealed in science fiction classics.

How can there be an imagination that is so truly vivid and compelling as that of Arthur C. Clarke? How was he able to conceive with great accuracy--years before their actual development—geosynchronous communications satellites, mobile communications satellites connecting to simple handsets, navigation satellites allowing universal accurate location, the Internet, artificial intelligence, Von Neumann machines, telecommuting, and bio-engineering. He has also envisioned everything from the birth control pill to e-commerce, from driverless cars to DNA testing. Perhaps most relevant of all he conceived of dozens of other futuristic technologies and applications that will perhaps someday soon be transformed from "magic" to "tomorrow's reality".

I had the opportunity—I won't say pleasure—to meet the Sci-Fi wizard Isaac Asimov in 1972 during the "Voyage beyond Apollo", at sea on the ocean liner S.S. Statendam. About 300 of us were cruising down from the Port of New York to Florida to see the last Moon Shot –Apollo 17. From there we continued on to Puerto Rico where no less than Carl Sagan gave us a tour of the Arecibo Radio Telescope. I can't say that Asimov was very pleasant. He certainly was not nearly as approachable as the dozens of other luminaries and cosmic geniuses on board such as Robert Heinlein, Ted Sturgeon, Roger Caras, Carl Sagan, and Norman Mailer. Even Katherine Anne Porter, of *Ship of Fools* fame, with her toy boy companion in tow, was easier to approach. I was amazed about how generous most of the scientific and literary stars on board were in their willingness to share time with a young space enthusiast.

But still, we must give Asimov his due. He was a damn fine spinner of tales. His *I Robot* and his *Foundation* trilogy represented creative true genius. Yet even he reluctantly acknowledged--when it came to "imaginative vision and predictive talent"-- he did not hold a candle to Sir Arthur.

Thus I can forgive Asimov for his lack of social graces if for no other reason than for having written the following line: "Nobody has done more in the way of enlightened prediction than Arthur C. Clarke." This he got exactly right. It is not only that Clarke made startling and accurate predictions about tomorrow's technology, but he always did this in an enlightened way that anticipated the economic, moral, social and philosophical implications as well. Clarke predicted mobile communications and mobile satellites, but at the same time he also anticipated that this could in time also be a true threat to our individual privacy. He even mused if ever there would be a time when it might be against the law to turn off our mobile devices.

Yet, in spite of the accuracy of Asimov's accolade, this laudatory blurb still managed to capture only a small part of the true visionary genius that was Arthur C. Clarke.

Merging the Left and Right Side of the Brain

Clarke's creative genius somehow always managed to capture the entire resources of both the left and the right hemispheres of his enormous brain--and to do so like no other. He was the full embodiment of what a human visionary could be. The breadth and depth of his soul was expressed in this always amazing human intellect that could so deftly balance scientific insight with speculative vision. He was uniquely able to capture the vast dimensions of the "entire human imagination". He was in a class all alone in how he could envision the past, the present and especially the future in the blink of an eye or with the click of his computer's mouse and also do so within the moral compass of what was right and wrong. He always seemed to grasp not only the future, but what that future should be. He had very strong views about clean oceans, green energy, the ecology, the evils of war, and the best aspirations for an improved human horizon. Then he could tie it up neatly in a bow with a succinct and often very witty epigram.

It seemed that his entire life was consumed with crafting yet another line of scientific questioning or a new and intriguing science fiction fantasy. He was always equally at ease with scientific fact and science fiction. He could switch from science to speculation on the turn of a dime and give you nine cents change. Virtually everything he wrote was rooted in scientific fact, engineering development or imaginative concepts ultimately destined to be tomorrow's reality. His one hundred or so books were divided almost half and half between science fiction and science fact.

There was this uncanny ability of Arthur C. Clarke to forecast the future brilliantly and with off-hand ease. The key seemed to be his unparalleled ability to blend together the mathematical left-hand side of his brain with his visionary and artistic right side as if they were a unified whole. Clarke, in short, could literally imagine the future like no other by peering beyond known science to envision the next quantum leap forward. This he often revealed with a brilliant gem that could be summed up in a single phrase or sentence.

Unexpected Developments	Expected Developments
X-Rays	Automobiles
Nuclear energy	Flying machines
Radio, TV	Steam engine
Electronics	Submarines
Photography	Spaceships
Sound recording	Telephones
Quantum mechanics	Robots
Relativity	Death rays
Transistors	Transmutation
Masers/Lasers	Artificial life
Atomic clocks/Mossbauer effect	Invisibility
Composition of celestial bodies	Levitation
Dating the past (Carbon 14, etc.)	Teleportation
Detecting invisible planets	Communication with dead
The Ionosphere	Observing the past
Van Allen Belts	Observing the future
	Telepathy

One of Arthur's greatest gifts was the ability to look at the future through the lens of a scientist and a seer with equal ease. His chart from *Profiles of the Future* (as above from page 26 of the book) breaks down new human capabilities into two groups. On one side he lists new, startling and unexpected capabilities that largely came through the efforts of scientists and engineers. On the other side are capabilities that futurists, science fiction writers, artists, folk lore spinners, and dreamers have anticipated and in some cases still think possible.

Clarke's genius was in not ruling out ideas or concepts that were channeled from the left or right side of his brain. Likewise he did not feel constrained by the limits of currently known technology. As he cheerfully advised, the way to progress forward was to venture forth from today's possible to into the world of tomorrow where the impossible might be achieved. He valued mystery and artistic insight on an equal par with scientific process, engineering and mathematics. This open mind allowed him to see the future with uncanny ability. Not many conventional scientists would be willing to contemplate how to go about achieving the last six items on the "expected list"—namely invisibility, levitation, teleportation, communication with the dead, observing the past or the future, or telepathy. To Clarke much that we can conceive is simply tomorrow's technology.

The Godfather

Arthur C. Clarke, more than any other person, should be considered as the Father of Satellite Communications. As he liked to say, he was perhaps the "Godfather" of the initial global satellite network known as Intelsat. I was a young executive at Intelsat when I first made contact with him some 35 years ago. In preparing for a global exhibit on telecommunications in Geneva, Switzerland on the occasion of the World Administrative Radio Conference of 1979, Gavin Trevitt and I approached him, on behalf of Intelsat, regarding a commemorative poster. We asked for his permission to create a poster featuring his May 25, 1945 four page paper entitled "The Space Station" that set forth how three satellites could create a set of virtual microwave towers that could cover the entire world's entire 360 degrees of longitude for radio services.

This May 25 article actually preceded his now famous *Wireless World* article in October 1945 about how three satellites in geosynchronous orbit (often known today as the Clarke Orbit) could provide global coverage to the world and effectively span the oceans more effectively than submarine cables—especially for broadcast services. To Clarke this was a very straightforward idea in terms of technological concept. He calculated that one would have to build a microwave tower hundreds of kilometers high to 'see' across the oceans, and this was an obvious non-starter in terms of cost and engineering. It was no great leap for him to imagine that a satellite relay at much higher altitude would do the same trick. He also explained that if you put this relay at high enough altitude and at the right orbital speed that matched the Earth's rotation it would indeed simulate a very tall "fixed" radio tower. The calculations that followed came up with an orbit that was some 35,786 kilometers (or 22,236 miles) above the Earth's surface or about 42,000 kilometers from the world's core. This he acknowledged was an orbit first identified by writer Hermann Noordung, whose original given name was Potocnik.

Clarke was amazingly open to the idea of the poster. Then he surprised us to say that not only was he willing to have Intelsat do the poster, but he even agreed to come to Geneva to sign the poster for everyone coming to the Intelsat booth. I still have a framed copy of that poster.

From that first encounter a lot transpired. I traveled to Colombo in Sri Lanka to visit Arthur. While I was there, Ambassador Wickremesinghe graciously organized a dinner at his home where Arthur's friends gathered to pay him tribute. The top leadership of the nation from business, the government and the legislature, the scientific community, all came to pay their respects. Everyone in Sri Lanka loved Arthur, Tamil and Sinhalese alike. The legislature passed the so-called "Arthur Act of 1976" to entice him to stay permanently in Sri Lanka.

Playing Ping Pong with Arthur

The highlight of that visit was my opportunity to play table tennis with Arthur at his home. My best result was 21-7—in Arthur's favor of course. I was not too abashed when I learned he was at the time the unofficial champion player of the country and certainly master at his local club where he played all comers and always won. And why was Arthur so good? The answer gives a useful insight into the man. He had a robot that could launch ping pong balls at nearly 70 miles an hour at different angles and elevations. It was against the robot that he practiced daily; if Arthur ventured into a project it was never by halfway measures.

And why was Arthur in Sri Lanka at all, since he was British through and through? He was born and raised in Somerset, England. He took over as head of farming at his home near Taunton, Somerset when he was just 13 after his father Charles died from lingering problems that came from breathing poisonous gas during World War I. Clarke, as the oldest of four siblings, had to bicycle 5 miles at 4am in the morning to go work at the Post Office sorting mail before going to school. He stayed on to complete his schooling at Huish School in Taunton, England. (The Arthur C. Clarke Foundation that I helped to start in 1983, today actually provides a Clarke Award to the top student at Huish School each year. The school still exists in downtown Taunton although it has moved to new, greatly expanded and more modern quarters and is known as The Richard Huish College.) Arthur and his three siblings helped out on the farm as well. It was far from an easy life for Mary Nora Willis Clarke and her four children after Charles Clarke's lingering death. The "C" in Arthur C. Clarke's name is indeed Charles after his father.

A King's College degree in Two Years

In short, Clarke grew up striving to survive and to be educated against the odds in rural England. He took the entrance examination for a post in Britain's Civil Service and he was 18 when he moved to London in 1936 to work in the accounts department of the Board of Education. He joined the British Interplanetary Society (BIS) and made many new friends. After a transfer to the department of Agriculture, he was moved to Wales and was fortunate to miss the heavy German bombing during the London Blitz. Then in 1942, he joined the armed forces with the Royal Air Force and began as a trainee at the RAF Radar School. He went on to work not only on conventional Royal Air Force systems but also with Luis W. Alvarez (who eventually worked on the Atomic Bomb) to develop automated RADAR assisted take-off and landing systems for aircraft. Clarke was far more than a one-act inventor.

But after World War II ended, Clarke understood that his vast brain needed more formal education and on October 7, 1946 he enrolled in

King's College, London, under a scholarship to get his bachelor of science degree. He had three fields of study: math, applied math and physics. This would have been a daunting task for anybody, but Arthur managed to complete a four year course of study in two years and come out with First Class Honors. During his studies he became particularly close to Professor McVittie, a well-known cosmologist and astronomer, who taught him math. Clarke reciprocated by teaching McVittie about rockets.

The Call of the Sea

From his childhood Clarke developed a boundless enthusiasm--not only for developing rockets and building telescopes that be began as a child--but also for exploring the oceans. After he left King's College with his degree he sought to travel the world. But his quest was not that of the typical tourist. His travels were directed at studying the oceans. Thus he was off to Florida, to the Great Barrier Reef of Australia and to the coast of Ceylon (now Sri Lanka) replete with his SCUBA gear in tow. He was born just three short blocks from the sea in the small resort town of Minehead, England, along the Bristol Channel. The oceans held a mighty grip on Arthur.

For most of the 1950s the lure of exploring the oceans dominated his life. From the time he built his first refractor telescope to the time he launched his first rocket, he was fascinated by space. But when his always cerebral brain calculated that he would not be able to go into space, he settled for the only foreign world he knew he could personally conquer—the oceans. During the 1950s he also quickly matured as a science fiction writer of note and began winning prizes for his work. _Childhood's End_ in 1953 launched him as a major star. Eventually he won every major award, including the Hugo, the Edgar, and many more.

His financial break-through, however, came when he was recruited by Stanley Kubrick to convert his short story 'The Sentinel' into the screenplay that was the basis for '2001: A Space Odyssey' that is now recognized by the American Film Institute in the top ten of all films ever made and the most highly rated science fiction movie of all time. Thus he finally bought a modest house in Ceylon (i.e. Sri Lanka) in the 1960s and in 1973 he moved into his Barnes Place mansion. This was the impressive 14 room estate that he bought from the Mother of the Bishop of Colombo, where he lived out the rest of his life. Then, in partnership with Hector Ekanayake, he founded "Underwater Safaris". By the time he had permanently settled there (after the Clarke Act of 1976 exempted him from paying taxes) he was indeed an established science fiction writer and in great demand all over the world.

Creating the Arthur C. Clarke Foundation

In 1983, on the occasion of World Communications Year, I had the opportunity to work with Arthur C. Clarke in a variety of ways. The first was the World Communications Year celebrations at the United Nations Headquarters in New York City. Arthur was invited, along with my boss, Santiago Astrain, then Secretary General of Intelsat, and officials of the International Telecommunications Union, to give keynote addresses.

In the meetings beforehand Arthur, in an unusually cheerful mood, casually agreed to a total of three significant requests that changed my life. He agreed to become the Honorary Chair of the Society of Satellite Professionals which was a brand new organization where I was serving as the organizing President. He also agreed to become associated with the new International Space University project that we were just beginning to organize. The three young founders of the Space Generation, Todd Hawley, Peter Diamandis and Robert Richards were there and were bursting with delight that Arthur C. Clarke would take them seriously. The third initiative was the proposal to create a new Arthur C. Clarke Foundation that would--among other things --provide educational assistance to students in South Asia. Today all three organizations have a global reach. There are now thousands of graduates from the International Space University and thousands of members of the Society of Satellite Professionals International.

Figure 1.1: Arthur C. Clarke and the Author Together at the United Nations in 1983

The Clarke Foundation has also undertaken a plethora of activities and initiatives that include founding of the Clarke Center for Human Imagination at the University of California at San Diego, a Clarke Institute for Space Science Education, museum exhibits and a number of awards and scholarships in the U.S. and the U.K.

I wish I could say that the idea to form the Foundation was mine. Actually it was a Sri Lankan Ph.D. student of mine at American University where I was at the time teaching in addition to my duties at Intelsat. Naren Chitty and I had talked to the Sri Lankan Ambassador de Alwis about this idea and we agreed that we would ask Arthur if he would allow us to proceed to form a Foundation in his name. That day in 1983 it seemed that Arthur would have said yes to any reasonable request. So in April 1983 at the White House which was the kick-off of the U.S. World Communications Year celebrations in the U.S. we handed out a press release and the Arthur C. Clarke Foundation was born. That day Buckminster Fuller came to the White House and gave one of his brilliant lectures, then traveled off to Chicago where he died just over a week later. Another of my idols gone but never forgotten.

But the White House celebrations were certainly a day to remember. Bill Ellinghaus, then the President of AT&T, appointed by President Reagan, served as Chairman of the U.S. World Communications Year Committee and I somehow ended up as Managing Director. As such I got to help write the President's speech. When I shook the hand of President Reagan and asked about the phenomenal achievements in the latest satellite technology that I had helped craft for the speech, the President could not recall the references he had made just a few minutes before. He delivered the words well but apparently did not fully   grasp their import. Anyway the White House ceremony and the reception at the State Department were both fabulous—and we still have the pictures to prove it.

In May we had the first meeting of the Arthur C. Clarke Foundation at Intelsat Headquarters, then located in L'Enfant Plaza in Washington, D.C. We were lucky to recruit former Secretary of the U.S. Air Force and President of Comsat General Corporation, Dr. John L. McLucas to chair the Foundation. John McLucas was a man of vision and had a great love for both space as well as Arthur C. Clarke. During his career John was the President of the American Institute of Aeronautics and Astronautics, the Administrator of the Federal Aviation Administration, Chair of the Board of the International Space University in addition to being Secretary of the Air Force and head of the National Reconnaissance Office. Other visionary space enthusiasts and executives we recruited to that Board included Dr. Elizabeth Young, Vice President of Comsat, Professor Edwin Parker of Stanford University, science fiction writer Ben Bova, Henry Herzheimer, President of Ford Aerospace Corporation, and Dr. Alfred "Bud" Whelon of Hughes Aircraft. Fred Durant, Assistant Director of the new Smithsonian National Air and Space Museum and long time close friend of Arthur, served as Executive Director and I served as Managing Director. Tedson Meyers, the current Chair of the Foundation, was our legal counsel who prepared the documents to file with the Internal Revenue Services to keep us legal as a non-profit organization.

We were off and running. Dr. John L. McLucas held the position as Chairman with distinction for almost two decades to provide the stature and stability we needed. We had also started something that would keep me in touch with Arthur C. Clarke, my idol and the king of the human imagination, for decades to come. All those involved were very happy campers indeed.

Why was Clarke Different?

Almost everyone who makes a lot of predictions can perhaps make one forecast about the future and get it right—but at the same time we might also get perhaps scores of them quite wrong. My personal batting average as a futurist is at best one in five. This still puts me up there with Jean Dixon and others that claim they can "see" the future. But Clarke was different. Many scores of times he was able to predict the future-- over a wide range of important areas--and he did so with uncanny detail and insight.

If one wishes to try to understand the concept of human imagination and try to unlock its meaning, then there is no better place to start than trying to get into the heart, soul and mind of Arthur—the eerily prescient man who saw an enlightened future and shared it with the world.

Arthur C. Clarke's Three Laws

Almost everyone who knows about Arthur C. Clarke tends to say: "Oh yes, Arthur C. Clarke and his three laws". These rules are at once humorous, quirky, insightful, and ultimately helpful in looking at all predictions of the future. These laws are as follows:

Arthur C. Clarke's Three Laws of Forecasting

Clarke's First Law: When a distinguished but elderly scientist states that something is possible, he is almost certainly right. When he states that something is impossible, he is very probably wrong. *(Arthur C. Clarke, "The Hazards of Prophecy: The Failure of Imagination" Profiles of the Future 1962, revised 1973, Harper & Row, paperback by Popular Library, ISBN 0-445-04061-0)*

Clarke's Second Law: The only way of discovering the limits of the possible is to venture a little way past them into the impossible. *(Arthur C. Clarke, "The Hazards of Prophecy: The Failure of Imagination" Profiles of the Future 1962, revised 1973, Harper & Row, paperback by Popular Library, ISBN 0-445-04061-0)*

Clarke's Third Law: Any sufficiently advanced technology is indistinguishable from magic. *(Arthur C. Clarke, "The Hazards of Prophecy: The Failure of Imagination" Profiles of the Future 1962, revised 1973, Harper & Row, paperback by Popular Library, ISBN 0-445-04061-0)*

One might conclude on the bases of these "laws of prediction" that Arthur C. Clarke is simply an entertaining writer with a quick wit. But, in fact, it was Clarke, who in 1945 fathered the key concepts of the geosynchronous communications satellite. During World War II he also played a role in the development of radar and the technology that today allows automated takeoff and landing of aircraft. His range of scientific and technical knowledge spanned oceanography, seismic activity of the Earth, a wide range of energy systems, artificial intelligence, space technology and systems, astrophysics and the workings of the solar system, the sun, the planets, asteroids, comets and the Moon, non-linear mathematics, fractals, and much more.. He was as fascinated with the Ocean as he was with space.

His three laws are actually helpful to anyone who makes a serious attempt to become a useful "futurist". Although it is not one of his "official" laws, it is important to note another one of his admonitions that could be considered a corollary to Laws 2 and 3. This was that anyone who seeks to make a long range forecast and to "get it right" needs to think boldly and come up with concepts that will be greeted as foolish and outrageous science fiction. **In short, any long range forecast that seems reasonable and well-conceived is likely to be wrong.**

Arthur C. Clarke: Author of Science Fact or Wizard of Science Fiction?

Yankee baseball player and humorist Yogi Berra was famous for a number of witticisms. One of his sayings was: "When you come to a fork in the road, take it." This was what Arthur C. Clarke did so well. He took the road of scientific analysis and invention. He then also took the road of science fiction and literary artistry. He took these divergent paths and married them with enormous skill that allowed science into his fiction. At the same time he used his fanciful and visionary brain to envision an amazing technological future.

The term 'science fiction' is important to note well when talking about Arthur. This is exactly what he wrote. If he was not writing science fiction then he wrote science fact. Nearly 50 of his 100 books were about rocketry, mathematics, ocean science, energy, or some other sector of the scientific world. Never did he abandon his science, regardless of which path he was following at the time. When he wrote *Reach for Tomorrow* in 1956, for instance, he explained that he had to carry out thirty pages of calculations to determine the orbits described in this novel. This was science fiction based on a heavy dose of science fact. These detailed early orbital mechanics calculations of launch mathematics also showed why electronic computers were essential for determining the correct pathways for rocket launches that were just a few years away.

Clarke was never one tempted to follow creative writers who wanted to change "SF" from science fiction into the fanciful and more emotional world of 'speculative fiction'—a world that had no requirement to be grounded in the real world of physics or science fact.

The solid scientific element of his fiction was central to understanding the special imaginative force of Clarke's writings. He believed that one could imagine alternative worlds, cultures and extraterrestrial events, but always within the realm of known physics. He was always "off put" by such things as Star Trek's "warp drive" that allowed space ships to travel at faster than the speed of light. Always, through an amazing global network of researchers and engineering gurus, he was seeking to learn the latest in chemistry, electro-magnetic phenomena, artificial intelligence, and other new fields of research. In all of his writings he was constantly connected to the latest scientific literature and probing the best minds on the planet. He was constantly in touch with those that were indeed exploring the unknown by scientific means. He subscribed to an amazing range of journals that one could find neatly arranged and catalogued in his upstairs library, office and lair for research and writing. This was a very large room on the second floor of Barnes Place with a ceiling fan for cooling that was eventually replaced by air conditioning.

And his research was not restricted to research journals, books and Internet sites. Arthur could pick up the phone and call someone like MIT Artificial Intelligence Lab Director Marvin Minsky to understand what capabilities a computer like HAL in the movie "2001: A Space Odyssey" might be expected to have. When he wanted to discuss large space platforms for advanced communications he called Ivan Bekey at NASA who headed programs in this area and there were many dozens more. He had one of the largest networks of engineers and genius on his call list of anybody in the world.

Arthur's amazing vision, new concepts and predictions were in large part pure Clarke-ism, but the other part was due to his dogged research and determination to get things right. This was a lesson he learned when he rode his bicycle to work at the Post Office at 4am at the age of 13.

Clarke spent most of his time in this upstairs room of his mansion located in the exclusive Cinnamon Gardens sector of downtown Colombo, Sri Lanka. Yet through satellite linkages and submarine cables he was connected to the world. A visit to his home on Barnes Place was always an adventure. On one visit I was subjected to a lecture on the importance of non-linear math and fractals. On another I was presented with a Hayes modem that had been fried by a bolt of lightning that I got fixed for free when I told the technician in a shop in Arlington, Virginia it was for Arthur C. Clarke. The oddest thing about the mansion is that when approaching it from the sedate street names Barnes Place it was an impressive and very sedate mansion. But drive along the commercial street, on the other side of the house and one could find display windows with mannequin divers in scuba diving gear promoting his company "Underwater Safaris".

Always Arthur was probing and seeking new answers. Sometimes it was the latest in satellite communications design or new levels of artificial intelligence capable of creative spontaneity. On one visit his laser-like attention was focused on the latest innovations in non-linear mathematics and Mandebrot two-dimensional fractal designs. He recognized early on how non-linear mathematics could be the key to understanding everything from patterns of evolution to stock market trends or coast line mapping. Then it was a fascination about desk-top atomic/chemical transactions as a possible future energy supply, and then it was on to the latest in earthquakes and tectonic plate shifts or the latest in oceanography research. One of his favorite lines was: "OTEC is the answer to OPEC". Translation: Ocean Thermal Energy Conversion (a new way to harvest energy from the sea) was the answer to the Organization of Petroleum Exporting Countries (OPEC).

The one constant was that he was never diverted too far away from scientific speculations about future worlds. He would never deign to embrace the alternative concept of "speculative fiction" such as literary fantasy writer Harlan Ellison has championed. Indeed one never knew exactly what Clarke, the polymath, was up to at any one time. He might be doing research for a serious scientific treatise on outer space, the oceans (about which he wrote as much as outer space), or on new alternative energy sources. Or his research on climate change might be for or doing his next science fiction novel or short story. Someday the myriad boxes of the so-called "Clarkives" will be opened and perhaps reveal a treasure trove of unpublished documents that will reveal the true diversity of Clarke's never-ending areas of research interests.

Today most of the treasure trove of "Clarkives" are on their way to the Smithsonian Air and Space Museum, but many of the boxes are tied with a red ribbon signaling that they are not to be opened until 50 years after his death.

Childhood's End was one of Arthur C. Clarke's earliest and most famous novels. The key focus of this story is a breakthrough in which all human children of a certain age learn how to achieve a "mind meld" in which they are able to link their minds together to create a global brain of incredible future intelligence. Clarke was candid in indicating that he was of two minds about the ending of the novel. Indeed he drafted alternative endings. The one he chose seemed to me rather bleak as the mind meld generation of young humanity was sealed off forever from their parents and all those that had come before.

Some might argue that the Internet and technology like IBM's Watson integrated computer software is taking us toward a "global brain" technology at a rapid rate. The question is whether all the brainpower of humanity will meld together or whether we will somehow just meld together our intelligent machines? These two quite different results would signal dramatically different futures for humanity.

The truth is that Arthur C. Clarke's brain was unique and integrative, but his large network of experts at the end of a phone was a sort of global brain at Clarke's disposal. Teilhard de Chardin, who in the 1900s wrote of an emerging "noosphere", anticipated that someday a network of linked information and knowledge would create a new Renaissance of knowledge. Clarke did much to create such a global knowledge network on which to test his flights of fancy.

Clarke's Predictions versus Modern Day Reality

This has all been preamble to what this book is all about -- The Imaginative Predictions of Arthur C. Clarke. This book explores exactly what he said when he made his predictions (Yesterday). Then we propose to compare his predictions with the technology, systems or software that is today's reality (Today). And finally we intend to examine his unrealized predictions to consider the current likelihood that they may ultimately be achieved (Tomorrow).

Some of these forecasts, such as the geosynchronous communications satellite that came from a conceptual and engineering-based analysis, are incredibly explicit and have come into existence largely as envisioned. This type of prediction was very concretely and explicitly realized and indeed now represents what is essentially over a $130 billion a year market. These rather explicitly engineered predictions will be examined first. Then we will move further and further into the future to examine Clarke's predictions in times yet to come

Chapter 2

Communications Satellites:
Fixed and Broadcast Space Stations

"A single station could only provide coverage to half the globe, and for a world service three would be required, though more could be readily utilized ....The stations would be arranged approximately equidistantly around the earth....Three satellite stations would ensure complete coverage of the globe. The stations in the chain would be linked by radio or optical beams, and thus any conceivable beam or broadcast service could be provided." **Arthur C. Clarke - "Extraterrestrial Relays: Can Rockets Stations Give World-Wide Radio Coverage?" - Wireless World,October, 1945.**

There is at least one purpose for which the [space] station is ideally suited and indeed has no practical alternative. This is the provision of world-wide ultra-high-frequency radio services, including television" **Arthur C. Clarke, in a letter - "The Space Station", May 25, 1945**

"An artificial satellite at the correct distance from the earth would make one revolution every 24 hours; i.e., it would remain stationary above the same spot and would be within optical range of nearly half the earth's surface. Three repeater stations, 120 degrees apart in the correct orbit, could give television and microwave coverage to the entire planet. I'm afraid this isn't going to be of the slightest use to our post-war planners, but I think it is the ultimate solution to the problem." **Arthur C. Clarke, "Peacetime Uses for V2" in <u>Wireless World</u>, March, 1945**

The two articles that Arthur C. Clarke wrote about communications satellites in *Wireless World,* as well as the letter that he circulated earlier in the year (June 1945), are remarkable in several ways. Most predictions or forecasts are rather vague or hazy presentations about the future that are couched in very broad and ambiguous terms. In this case, Clarke was presenting the case as to why a new and yet undeveloped technology could evolve from systems and technology currently underway. He also explained why this particular new application of space—namely the geosynchronous orbit--made good business sense and could fulfill a vital need. The four page article in October 1945 was not only highly cogent, but set forth all aspects of the key technical background needed to deploy future satellite networks. Thus Clarke noted that the   German war-time V2 rocket technology could be extended to launch satellites into low earth orbit without a great deal of new development. He explained the orbital positions that ultimately might make sense for a global satellite network for radio and television broadcast and distribution at the much higher and difficult to achieve geosynchronous orbits. He even noted that the frequencies that might be used could be anything from microwave radio frequencies up to light (laser) transmission systems.

The question that might spring to mind is why did Arthur foresee communications satellite services being many decades in the future when in fact service began on the Intelsat system just twenty years later in 1965? I had a chance to discuss this with him at his home in Sri Lanka.

He noted from his calendar journal for the year that he received only 15 pounds sterling (about $60 at the time) in compensation for his article in *Wireless World* in 1945. This does seem a paltry sum for what was to turn into a multi-billion dollar industry. He explained that the reason he did not attempt to patent and profit from the idea was because radio wave transmissions in 1945 depended on conventional radio tube amplifiers and that these burned out with considerable frequency. The reason Clarke referred to "rocket stations" deployed perhaps 50 to 100 years in the future was that he envisioned that these stations would need to have crew aboard who would be responsible for installing new radio tubes as the operating radio amplifiers died.

Yet Clarke remained philosophical about his miscalculation as to when global communications satellites would go into service by writing an article entitled: "How I Lost a Billion Dollars in My Spare Time". In this article in his 1992 book _How the World Was One_ he explained how quickly he had scribbled down the original ideas thusly: " I risked nothing except a few hours of my time; but other men have risked their reputations and their careers....the people that deserve the real credit for communications satellites are those who had to convert my paper plans into hardware that would function flawlessly for months and years on end, thousands of miles above the earth."

It was during the period 1947 to 1951 that John Bardeen, Walter Brattain and William Shockley developed the new transistor technology that led to today's solid state amplifiers. Now we have silicon and gallium arsenide monolithic devices that can support communications satellites that operate 15 to 18 years in orbit without failure. Even traveling wave tubes, which were developed by Rudolf Kompfner--and were critical to the earliest satcoms—were just coming out of the laboratory when Clarke published his original articles quoted above. It was also the transistor that allowed the development of modern computers that can crunch the numbers for launch operations and the orbital mechanics key to satellite launches.

In short, Clarke had the orbits, the satellite locations, the transmission medium, the deployment method all correct. He even foresaw the use of laser inter-satellite links to interconnect satellites. The May 25 1945 article even anticipated spot beams and very small aperture terminals that were 30 centimeters in size. He predicted that satellites could also be used for navigation and weather forecasting as well. The only aspect he did not conceive of was transistors and monolithically integrated circuits to allow the creation of solid-state circuits and amplifiers that would boost reliability and eliminate the need to constantly replace burnt out radio tubes.

He published a book just a few weeks before the launch of Sputnik in 1957 called _The Making of a Moon_ about how to design and launch artificial satellites into orbit as human's first venture into space. In this book he wrote: "It may seem premature, if not ludicrous to talk about the commercial possibilities of satellites, yet the airplane became of commercial importance within thirty years of its birth, and there are good reasons for thinking that this time scale may be shortened in the case of the satellite, because of its immense value in the field of communications."

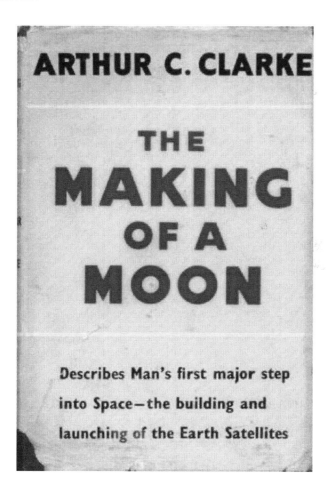

Figure 2.1: Arthur's Guide to Building and Launching Satellites

Just three weeks after this book on building satellites appeared the world of outer space changed for real. On October 4, 1957, the world was stunned by the launch of the world's first artificial satellite as part of the 1957-1958 International Geophysical Year. This single event, the launch of a small satellite the size of beach ball, changed the geopolitical landscape of the world in a large way. It certainly kick-started a major space effort in the United States. While this Soviet launch startled most people it certainly did not come as a surprise to Sir Arthur who had anticipated this day for decades.

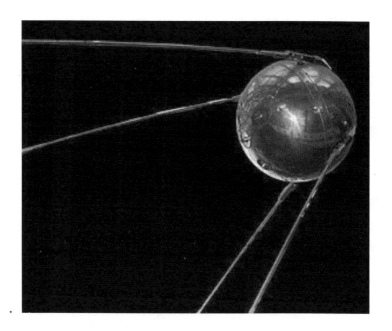

Figure 2.2: Sputnik 1--The World's First Artificial Satellite

Clarke certainly understood that the practical use of space would change the world. He wrote: "Comsats will end ages of   isolation, making us all members of a single family....Thanks to a few tons of electronic gear twenty three thousand miles above the equator, ours will be the the last century of the Savage; and for all mankind, the Stone Age will be over."

And the world did begin to change rapidly. Not only did the Soviet Union and the United States begin to develop experimental communications satellites but a process to create a mechanism to cooperate in space and develop commercial satellite ventures came on the heels of the launch of Sputnik. President John F. Kennedy had these words to say when the Communications Satellite Act of 1962 was passed by Congress after extended debate as to whether this technology should be developed as a public or private enterprise:

"The benefits which a satellite system should make possible within a few years will stem largely from a vastly increased capacity to exchange information cheaply and reliably with all parts of the world by telephone, telegraph, radio and television. The ultimate result will be to encourage and facilitate world trade, education, entertainment and new kinds of professional, political and personal discourse which are essential to healthy human relationships and international understanding"– *(President John F. Kennedy on signing the Communications Satellite Act of 1962)*

A year earlier in 1961, the newly-elected President Kennedy had made his speech about going to the Moon and coming back within the decade. He had also announced a major funding initiative to develop communications satellites. When he then said: "We intend to go to the Moon, and to do the other things…" he meant comsats and weathersats.

While the U.S.S.R. was clearly ahead in launch vehicle technology, it turns out that the U.S. was more adept at developing new space applications. Among the first of the U.S. launches were many experimental communications satellites. These included SCORE (1958), Echo (1960), Telstar (1962) and Relay (1962). But it was the launch of Syncom 2 into geosynchronous orbit in 1963 that tangibly realized Arthur C. Clarke's prediction of a global satellite network in this special orbit that we now call the "Clarke Orbit".

Figure 2.3: Syncom 2 was the World's First Geosynchronous Communications Satellite (courtesy of the Comara Comsat Legacy Program)

This landmark satellite was designed by Dr. Harold Rosen and his team at Hughes Aircraft Corporation and launched by NASA after the attempted launch of Syncom 1 failed.

In just 18 years Clarke's prediction had made the transition from "wild-eyed fantasy" to experimental reality. In another two years the first operational geosynchronous satellite made its debut. Yet another seminal prediction by Arthur C. Clarke was fulfilled.

Thus the launch of the world's first commercial satellite, Early Bird, occurred on April 6, 1965, just twenty years after Arthur C. Clarke's ground breaking articles. By today's standards this satellite was a mere minnow among whales. It weighed less than 40 kilograms and had a peak power of less than100 watts. Nevertheless it was able to provide a throughput of 240 voice circuits or the equivalent of one low quality black and white television channel. The largest voice submarine cable of its day only commanded 72 voice circuits.

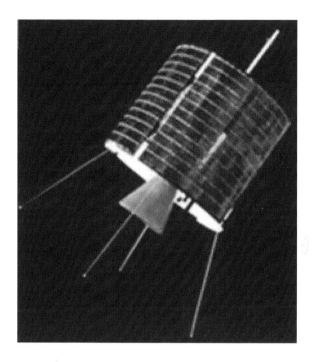

Figure 2.4: Early Bird: The World's First Commercial Satellite - Launched in 1965
(courtesy of Comara and the Comsat Legacy Program)

This satellite, officially known as Intelsat 1 (F-1), was thus a giant among the transoceanic telecommunications links of its day. It set the stage for a tremendous surge in satellite technology and for the accomplishments that followed in the next fifty years. The USSR also launched its Molniya satellites in 1965. It required three of these satellites in highly elliptical orbits to provide continuous coverage of the northern latitudes of this vast country. Yet these large and massive satellites provided less effective coverage and large ground antennas with tracking ability were required to follow them in orbit.

The U.S. military, in yet a third approach to satellite communications service, deployed what it called the Initial Defense Satellite Communications System (IDSCS). When one compared the cost of these various types of satellites, the cost of the tracking earth stations, and their performance, it became clear to everyone that Arthur C. Clarke's concept for satellite communications made by far the best sense. Early Bird was designed, tested, and launched for under $9 million dollars. Clearly the successful Early Bird launch vindicated the geosynchronous satellite design concept and indicated that the Comsat Corporation's initial capitalization through an Initial Public Offering (IPO) in the amount of $200 million had actually been overcapitalized.

The following years were filled with one major innovation after another. Platform stability via 3-axis body stabilized de-spun antennas allowed satellite antennas to be constantly pointed toward the Earth to increase performance. High-powered and accurately pointed spot beams that had also been predicted by Clarke were deployed on the Intelsat IV satellites in 1971. These beams allow more capacity and frequency reuse. This new technology, all of which had been anticipated by Clarke, allowed satellite capacity to jump from 240 voice circuits to 4000 voice circuits plus two high quality television channels—a jump in satellite capability of 20 times in a period of just six years. This amazing innovation, spot beams, made possible via large aperture satellite antennas and precise pointing accuracy from spinning and then 3-axis body stabilized platforms have provided one of the most important   keys to satellite advances over the last few decades.

And which of these innovations did Arthur C. Clarke overlook? All one has to do is examine the illustration in the "Extra Terrestrial Relays" article in _Wireless World_ to see a clear presentation of what else but spot beams! His Extra-Terrestrial Relays article clearly stated: "Larger reflectors could be used to illuminate single countries or regions for the more restricted services with consequent economy of power. On the higher frequencies it is not difficult to produce beams less than a degree in width."

At the end of this book in the appendices is a detailed evaluation of Clarke's two 1945 articles on communications satellites by a fan named Sven from the European Space Agency. He finds 38 detailed predictions that Clarke made in these two articles and concludes at least 25 have come true and 7 are arguable - or at least half true. Not a bad average for any futurist or seer.

The march of satellite technology since the 1970s has continued unabated. Innovations of note have included the development of the three-axis body stabilized platform using high speed momentum wheels. These high speed wheels (i.e. devices that spin at 4000 to 5000 revolutions per minute) whirl as if they are a very high speed top. These devices allow the satellite platform to maintain precise pointing of increasingly larger antennas. This design also allows the constantly pointing of solar cell arrays toward the sun. Other key developments over the last 50 years include better solar cells (e.g. Gallium Arsenide), better batteries (e.g. Lithium ion), on-board signal processing and switching (i.e. to better interconnect spot beams), higher performance modulator/demodulators (modems) and coder/decoders (codecs), advanced digital multiplexing and deployable and un-furlable antennas that can now well exceed 20 meters (i.e. over 70 feet in diameter).

The greatest advances in all forms of radio communications, however, have come through digital communications. This development has allowed the use of digital encoding so that more information can be crammed into the available radio frequencies. Just a few years ago a communications satellite was transmitting information in the microwave band at a typical rate of one bit per hertz (a hertz, named after Heinrich Hertz, means a cycle/second). Today transmission rates of up to six bits per hertz are achievable through advanced coding techniques such as so-called Turbocoding. The trend is for advanced satellites to perform as advanced digital processing systems in the sky. Thus satellites today have specialized software that allows them to transmit and receive communications with great efficiency.

The remarkable development of satellite communications over the past thirty years has allowed for these devices to become more complex, capable, and powerful so that the ground systems can be made simpler, smaller, less costly and still support a wide range of services. When satellite services began with Early Bird, the Intelsat Standard A Earth Stations weighed 10 to 20 tons, were staffed by a 24/7 crew of perhaps 60 to 70 people, and these huge devices cost tens of millions of dollars (in un-inflated dollars). Today's two-way user terminals can be hand held phones, units that look like laptop computers, or so-called very small aperture terminals (VSATs) that might be something like 1-3 meter dishes. Receive only television dishes for direct broadcast satellites can be as small as just 33 centimeter (1 foot) dishes and these devices cost only a few hundred dollars installed. This technology inversion has led to satellites that have become bigger and more complex as ground stations have shrunk from gigantic and expensive behemoths to small consumer devices. This is one of the great technological triumphs of electronics and computer systems in the 20th and 21st centuries.

The tremendous development of satellite technology, coupled with digital communications and the Internet (which Arthur also envisioned), has allowed an enormous range of new technologies to develop. A great diversity of satellite services are provided to commercial markets and it is not unreasonable to conclude that the over $200 billion (U.S.) in annual revenues that derive from space applications can all be traced directly or indirectly to Arthur Clarke's first predictions.

The story of the evolution of communications satellites is far from ended. The latest evolutionary step has come with high throughput satellites that can operate with hundreds of spot beams and transmit trillions of bits per second. The highly focused beams, like spotlight beams, accomplishes several objectives. The concentration of the beam width means less spreading out of the signal so that it is more concentrated when it reaches Earth after traveling the huge distance from geo orbit. This allows the user terminal to be smaller and less costly, also allowing the reuse of the same frequencies over and over again in a repeating pattern. This is because the circular areas on the ground that these satellite beams are illuminating are separated far enough from one another to not interfere. Each one of the satellite beams in the most capable satellites can send billions of bits of information per second and so the satellites have very high total digital throughput to support television, voice, data transmission, etc.

When the first satellites were developed separate antennas were used to create each beam with the feed system that generated the radio beam right in the very center of the parabolically-shaped antenna reflector. When the designers decided they needed to create a very large number of beams they came up with a new idea. That idea was to create one very large antenna reflector and then devise a complex radio feed system that could bounce many different beams off the reflector at slightly different angles. This technology is known as a multi-beam antenna and it is the basis of today's very high throughput satellites.

There has been enormous progress in satellite technology and performance since Arthur C. Clarke first conceived of global networks in the sky, but the full potential of these networks are still to be realized. There are many new concepts that could take satellites to new heights, if one might pardon the pun. There are concepts such as large scale inflatable antennas. The use of so-called phased array feed systems could be used to create electronically shaped beams which might even be formed off of very large scale "flat antenna structures" or "adaptive membrane" antenna structures. With this type of antenna design it might be possible to create not just hundreds of beams but thousands of very narrow beams the size of a large terrestrial cellular beam. Such a satellite with thousands of beams might reuse frequencies many hundreds of different times and boost satellite throughput to trillions of bits per second in order to achieve transmission rates equivalent to the fiber-optic laser transmission systems. Some of the various satellite technologies of the future that might realize Arthur C. Clarke's most advanced concepts for satellite technology that would include high throughput communications between the Moon and Earth (i.e. so-called cislunar links).

Conclusions

To date communications satellites have increased from 240 voice circuits (Early Bird) to at least 6 million voice equivalent circuits (ViaSat 1). This is an increase in transmission throughput of some 4000 times in 50 years. Who is to say that similar progress will not be made in another half century? But if in 2065 we are actually in need of satellite space stations each with 24 billion voice equivalent circuits (or about 50 million digital television channels) our problem may not be with communications but with coping with over population, information overload and frequency congestion.

Chapter 3

Cellular and Mobile Satellite Services

"The old science fiction dream of the wrist watch telephone could soon come true, and at a cost of a few dollars—given the determination to achieve it. Can you imagine the impact the impact of this upon societies where, at present there is only one telephone per thousand people? Sometime during the century, the human race will become one big, gossiping family." **Arthur C. Clarke Address to the UNESCO Conference on the International Programme on the Development of Communications (IPDC), Paris, France, June 1981.**

"It might even make possible world-wide person-to-person radio with automatic dialing. Thus no one on the planet need ever get lost or become out of touch with the community, unless he wanted to be. I am still thinking about the social consequence of this." **Letter from Arthur C. Clarke to Andrew Haley, of the British Interplanetary Society August 1956.**

"One of the disadvantages of universal [mobile] communications will be the loss of privacy. Within a very few years, the long-heralded dream (or nightmare) of the wristwatch radiophone will be upon us: Given a man's number, you will be able to call him anywhere on Earth, even if you have no idea where he is…..one only hopes that the time never comes when it is a criminal offense to switch off your personal receiver." **Arthur C. Clarke, "Everybody in Instant Touch: The Coming of the Space Age", Meredith Press, New York (1967).**

"For all of its obvious advantages, the fixed synchronous satellite has one unavoidable defect…..it takes an appreciable time…..even if your listener answers immediately, it will be just over a half second before you can receive his reply….To overcome this problem, it may be necessary to establish communications satellites much closer to the Earth than the synchronous orbit. Such systems will require numerous satellites, and elaborate ground antennas to track them as they move rapidly across the sky." **Arthur C. Clarke, _"Everybody in Instant Touch: The Coming of the Space Age"_, Meredith Press, New York (1967).**

One of the most fundamental shifts in human interactions and social intercourse has come about by the mobile communications revolution that has unfolded since the 1970s. As is par for the course Arthur C. Clarke anticipated not only the technology but also the impact that it will make on our lives in terms of privacy and immediacy of interaction. He also anticipated how this will impact the nature of work, telecommuting and other such things that we will address in later chapters. In such books as _How the World Was One_ and other publications he anticipated a world in which global mobile communications would be a major feature of modern life. On the previous page are just four of his prophetic statements beginning in 1956.

The Rise of Cell Phone Technology for Urban Mobile Communications

The great limitation of car phone service in its early days was that it was available to only very wealthy and politically powerful people in the United States and around the world. Its development was constrained by the lack of radio frequency spectrum. The technology that changed this was developed by American Telephone and Telegraph's Bell Labs. The idea was to create small "cells" in a repeating pattern so that specifically assigned frequencies could be used over and over again. This so-called approach of frequency re-use was developed in late 1970s and the early 1980s. This is how we ended up with the name "cellular" or "cellphone" service. The initial systems, as reviewed and endorsed by the National Academy of Science and the National Academy of Engineers, used relatively large cells and analog-based multiplexing technology. In a relatively short period of time, however, the cells shrunk in size, digital multiplexing was introduced, and then frequencies were reallocated to this use as mobile services gained great popularity.

By the 1990s mobile cellular use had become the fastest growing service in telecommunications history. At the start of the 1990s cellular mobile telephone service was characterized by only limited link margins (i.e. limited ability to provide extra power if something was blocking the signal), limited spectrum allocations and spotty coverage in many locations. This early service represented a newly emerging market that concentrated on early adopters and those with a real need for mobile connectivity. But by the end of the decade in 2000, cellular phone service in the U.S., Canada, Europe, Japan and even countries like South Korea and Russia was challenging conventional landline service in number of subscribers. Suppliers of cell phones were producing hundreds of millions of handsets a year and technical innovations were making these amazing devices smaller, more capable, and affordable year by year, if not month by month. The type of service that Clarke envisioned in the 1950s had come to pass in terms of terrestrial cellular mobile service based on neighborhood cell towers that spread not only across cities but along Interstate highways, train routes, and suburban and exurban amoebas of development. Today, rather amazingly, there are more cellphones in the United States than there are people. The success of terrestrial cellular service led to plans to offer this service by satellite as well.

LBJ and the Early Days of Car Phones

Back in the 1950s and 1960s the story about wireless communications was dramatically different than it is today. When Arthur C. Clarke was making his predictions about the development of terrestrial and satellite mobile communications, there was very limited radio communications available. This land-based radio service was largely used for the dispatch of taxi-cabs and for similar types of business communications services. It was very difficult and expensive for individuals to obtain mobile radio communications services. However, the U.S. Senate Majority Leader Lyndon Baines Johnson (before he became U.S. President) had such a prized mobile phone service in Washington, D.C. The probably apocryphal story is that a rival Senator, after years of waiting, finally got a mobile radio communications line and called Johnson on his car phone to brag he had managed to get this exclusive service too. Johnson, who always had a wry and sometimes rough sense of humor, interrupted to say: "Sorry I have to hang up, I have a call coming in on my other car phone line."

Satellite Communications Services for Maritime, Aeronautical and Outside the City

An entirely separate track was taken for mobile satellite services. Since clearly terrestrial cell towers would simply not work at sea, maritime mobile satellite services seemed like a very logical way for satellite networks to expand. Thus in the 1970s attention turned to using satellite systems for connection to ships at sea. Lots of different opportunities presented themselves in what turned out to be quite a jumble of different approaches. A satellite network, known as Marisat, was indeed the first marine mobile satellite system and it was designed by the Communications Satellite Corporation (Comsat) for the U.S. Navy and built by Hughes Aircraft. Half of the capacity on the three Marisat satellites was reserved by the US Navy and the half left over was made available for Comsat (through its commercial subsidiary Comsat General) to sell commercially. The first of the Marisat systems went up in 1973. The European Satellite Agency (ESA) developed an "experimental satellite" known as MARECS (this stood for Maritime European Communications Satellite). Then the Intelsat Organization included a Maritime package that flew on the Intelsat V-7, -8 and -9 satellites.

At one time Intelsat officials thought that they might provide all types of satellite services on an integrated system, but this was not to be. In 1979, all of this very diverse mobile maritime satellite capability was made available to the newly created Inmarsat Organization, that was set up after some complicated international negotiations. Inmarsat (short for the International Maritime Satellite Organization) was established as an entirely new international organization for maritime mobile satellite communications. This organization, patterned in large part on Intelsat, was established in London, United Kingdom.

Although the Intelsat Organization (the International Telecommunications Satellite Organization) had the possibility within its charter to provide so-called "specialized services" that included maritime and aeronautical satellite services, there were several forces at work that led to the Inmarsat solution. The countries that had major maritime fleets and thus had the largest maritime communications needs were clearly differentiated from the largest users of Intelsat. Norway, Panama, and Liberia had only a modest participation in Intelsat and the USSR (i.e. Russia) was entirely on the outside looking in. The British Commonwealth countries—led by Australia and the United Kingdom - also felt they wanted a larger say in the new Inmarsat organization than they had in Intelsat. These maritime users were not really happy with the idea that they would be restricted to their service needs being met by hosted payloads operated on Intelsat satellites. In short the maritime countries did not really relish the idea that their mobile communications needs and their voting power, with regard to future satellite networks, would always be relegated to "second fiddle" within the existing Intelsat organization, which at that time was dominated by the U.S. and in particular by the U.S Signatory, the Communications Satellite Corporation.

The Inmarsat organization when it came into being in 1979 had to somehow mesh these three quite different satellite systems and capabilities and to try to provide an integrated global network for maritime mobile services. The only things these three quite diverse capabilities had in common were frequencies and orbits. Since all of this satellite capacity was deployed in geosynchronous systems they all were limited by significant transmission delays. Users were faced with about a half second for a round trip to geo orbit and back for the first talker and then the same distance for the second talker to reply. This is the problem that Arthur C. Clarke had noted in his 1967 speech.

Inmarsat immediately began to design an integrated network that ultimately resulted in new networks over the next three decades called the Inmarsat 1, 2, 3 and now Inmarsat 4 and Inmarsat Xpress satellites. All of these satellites have been deployed in geosynchronous orbit because of the economic efficiencies that Clarke had noted from the outset.   The design of the new generation of Inmarsat satellites included ever more capable and larger spacecraft antennas that allowed each new generation of satellite to mimic the terrestrial cellular systems by creating smaller and smaller beams with more and more frequency reuse and the ability to work to smaller and lower cost user terminals. In short the many beams from the satellite in the sky can now mimic the types of beams created by terrestrial cellular systems on the ground. The key reason for this cellular beam structure—in the sky or on the ground—is to be able to use the limited radio frequencies over and over again.

One of the Inmarsat 4 satellites, first deployed in 2005, is pictured below in Figure 3.1. This giant satellite has a huge 10 meter deployable parabolic antenna with a wing tip span of 45 meters - almost the length of an Olympic sized swimming pool. It has a complete feed system that allows a complicated and dense pattern of many different beams to bounce off the surface of the antenna. This actually allows the creation of 220 different spot beams, over twenty regional beams and even global coverage beams, all by using so-called multi-beam satellite antenna technology. This single satellite can thus become the equivalent of nearly seventy cell towers on the ground, since terrestrial cell towers typically project out only four different beams at a time.

Figure 3.1: Inmarsat 4 Satellite with Giant Antenna in Geo Orbit (Graphic courtesy of Inmarsat)

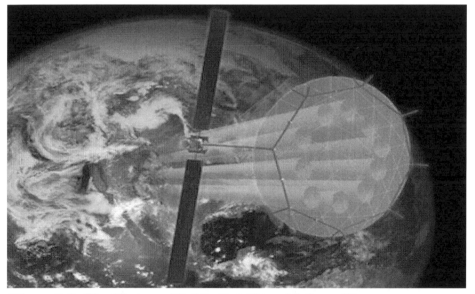

Figure 3.2: The Skyterra Mobile Satellite with huge 22 meter Deployable Antenna (Graphic courtesy of Harris Corporation).

Since the Inmarsat 4 satellites were deployed even larger satellite antennas have been built and deployed by the Harris Corporation for mobile satellite services, designed to work interactively with terrestrial mobile cellular systems. The largest of these, as shown in figure 3.2 below, were 22 meters (or 72 feet) in diameter and covers a total area equivalent in size to a large chunk of a football field.

Solving the Problem of Transmission Delays

Arthur Clarke, in his first predictions about mobile satellites as noted above, explained that there could be a few problems with using the geosynchronous orbit for this service. He noted that for true mobile satellite service to be effective for a user on the ground the transceiver device would have to be small and not require much power and be low in cost. He also suggested that the transmission delays of a quarter of a second to go one way and a half of second to complete a round trip could also be a problem—especially if the user was engaged in something urgent as might be the case for a fire or police first responder. This is why he suggested that a different type design might be employed. His suggestion of a low earth orbit constellation that would involve a large number of satellites transmitting their signals down might be a possible answer.

Once again Arthur was right on the mark. Two of the first mobile satellite networks that were deployed in the late 1990s were the so-called Iridium Mobile Satellite network and the Globalstar Mobile Satellite network. The Iridium satellite constellation network that went up in 1997 consisted of sixty-six satellites plus spares to provide satellite beams suited to operate with hand-held user terminals on the ground. This was closely followed by the Globalstar network deployed the following year. This network was in a somewhat higher orbit and had 48 satellites plus spares. It too was designed to operate to user terminals that were only slightly larger than a cell phone. Since these satellites were thirty to forty times closer to the Earth than a Geo orbit satellite, their communications had thirty to forty times less delay and the beams from the satellite spread out much, much less by the time that they traveled to the Earth's surface. Since radio transmission beams spread out in a circle, the so-called "path loss" of the signal relates not to the distance the satellite is away from Earth but to the square of the distance. This means that if the antenna on a Geo satellite is the same size as the antenna on a low earth orbit satellite that is 30 times closes the effective performance is not 30 times stronger but 30 x 30 or effectively 900 times stronger.

The backers of the Iridium and Globalstar networks thought that this type of service would be extremely popular and that there would be millions of subscribers world-wide willing to pay a significant monthly fee to stay in touch around the globe. Unfortunately this did not turn out to be the case. This lack of significant demand was for several reasons. These included the difficulty of attaining connections inside of buildings or cars or truck by satellite phone and the comparative larger size and higher prices of the satellite phones. The biggest reason of all, however, was the many competitive improvements that had been made in ground-based cellular services in the seven to ten years it took to license, design, build and launch these new systems.

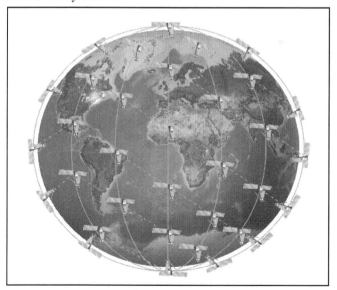

Figure 3.3: Iridium Global Mobile Satellite Constellation in LEO Orbit

In short, in the 1970s there was an enormous extension and power boost for terrestrial cellular systems throughout many developed economies. The power boost for the terrestrial systems over the ten year period that satellite networks were being planned and constructed allowed reliable ground cellular connectivity to be achieved in many countries across a wide sweep of towns, cities, and along major highways and train lines. This allowed the terrestrial cell phones to become smaller, cheaper and more convenient since they now worked much more reliably inside of buildings and inside vehicles.

It turned out that armed forces in the field, peacekeepers in remote areas and people with employment that took them far away from cities into rural areas did want this type of mobile satellite service, but the rapid build out of terrestrial cellular in urban areas and along railroads and interstate highways effectively undercut the much broader satellite market. Ground based cellular systems built thousands more towers, deployed better digital technology and became more reliable by boosting power margins by more than hundreds to even thousands of times. The satellite market in the millions did not materialize for the low earth orbit systems and three networks designed on the basis of constellations—namely Iridium, Globalstar, and later ICO -- all went bankrupt in the late 1970s. What seemed so very promising as a gigantic new and lucrative satellite market in the mid to late 1980s had shrunk into a much smaller yet still significant market in the early 2000s.

This "recalibrated" mobile satellite market was re-aimed largely at military, police, firefighters and workers in remote areas plus systems designed for ships at sea and for airplanes. It turned out this market could indeed be served not only by lower earth orbit satellite constellations but also by GEO satellites with very large aperture antennas—at least up to 50 degrees latitude. These large aperture satellite beams on huge satellites such as the Inmarsat 4 could concentrate power to serve the market and the delay problem could be adjusted to by many users such as first responders and military personnel. Today there are thus both types of systems, i.e. Geo and Leo systems. The Geo mobile satellite networks are called Inmarsat and Thuraya. In addition there is the reorganized Iridium business, with a reconstituted system that operates the original network under new management and ownership. Currently Iridium is building and deploying an improved design and more powerful satellite in a low earth orbit constellation called Generation NEXT. Clarke was thus again right in anticipating that a combination of satellite technologies in both Geo and Leo orbits might be needed to serve the markets of the future. Today mobile satellites are creating technology niches that seem to need satellites of both types with Leo constellations being key to communications in the higher latitudes

Conclusions

The huge challenge in fulfilling the next generation of growth in mobile communications seems to be the adequate supply of spectrum for terrestrial broadband mobile services and/or satellite broadband mobile services. Studies conducted in Europe, the U.S., Canada, and Japan project annual growth in demand for new mobile services—particularly wideband video-related services—as high as 40% per year. Digital coding efficiencies to allow more bits per unit of bandwidth to be transmitted seems to be part of the answer. The reallocation of frequencies from traditional over-the-air television transmission will likely be another part of the story, but nothing can grow by 40% per year for ever. New solutions such as increasingly smaller cells (sometimes called pico-cells) or more efficient ways of transmitting video information will be needed. Some project the stabilization of population growth around 2050 could also help slow rates of growth for mobile services that today are the most rapidly growing type of communications or IT service. For years broadcast and fixed satellite communications have dominated global satellite applications revenues and with the most rapid growth, but today the constant demand for more and more mobile services, including video streaming to mobile devices, have boosted satellite-based mobile services and it is likely that mobile demand will rise the fastest in coming decades.

Chapter 4

Navigation Satellites

"...three satellites in the 24-hour orbit could provide not only an interference and censorship-free global tv service for the same power as a single modern transmitter, but could also make possible a position-finding grid whereby anyone could locate himself by means of a couple of dials on an instrument the size of a watch." **Arthur C. Clarke, Wireless World, October 1945.**

"...he [Q] suggested the Brick Moon. The plan was this: If from the surface of the earth, by a gigantic peashooter, you could shoot a pea upward from Greenwich, aimed northward as well as upward; if you drove it so fast and far that when its power of ascent was exhausted, and it began to fall, it should clear the earth, and pass outside the North Pole; if you had given it sufficient power to get it half round the earth without touching, that pea would clear the earth forever...... If only we could see that pea as it revolved in that convenient orbit, then we could measure the longitude from that, as soon as we knew how high the orbit was, as well as if it were the ring of Saturn. But a pea is so small!" "Yes," said Q., "but we must make a large pea." Then we fell to work on plans for making the pea very large and very light.... It must stand fire well, very well. Iron will not answer. It must be brick; we must have a [hollow] Brick Moon." - **Edward Everett Hale, "The Brick Moon", Atlantic Monthly, Oct. Nov. Dec., 1869**.

Arthur C. Clarke's genius was in part his ability to mine the intellectual and scientific writings of the past and discover important nuggets that have been overlooked and forgotten. In his suggestion of the geosynchronous orbit for a global communications network he recognized the importance of the Slovenian writer Hermann Noordung (1892-1929) who was born Herman Potocnik. Noordung, who was a thinker and writer of cosmonautics, first suggested that space stations might be launched in geosynchronous orbit but not as means of global communications. Clarke likewise recognized that Edward Everett Hale in his short story "The Brick Moon" had identified a logical way to employ orbiting satellites of known orbital parameters to calculate longitude and latitude and that multiple satellites that were visible worldwide would be necessary to accomplish this task. Clearly satellites of much higher orbits, like the Geo orbit, would be more efficient than the 4000 miles (6400 kilometers) orbit that Hale had indicated in his short story.

Perhaps the most remarkable part of Clarke's prediction was the thought that an instrument the size of a watch would be able to tell future navigators exactly where they were in terms of longitude and latitude. It is indeed due to today's application specific integrated circuits (ASICs) that it is indeed possible to have a small handheld unit that can calculate exact locations. In the case of Edward Everett Hale's concept of a Brick Moon, the idea was to be able to physically "see" the giant "pea" in the sky and measure how much above the horizon it circled. Arthur C. Clarke's concept that involved a geosynchronous satellite circling out--a tenth of the way out to the Moon--was clearly not based on sight, but rather radio signals and calculation of transmission times to determine locations for navigation. What was particularly unique about Clarke's forecast with regard to navigation satellites was anticipating that the device for accurate navigation could, in fact, be as small as a wrist watch. Today smart phones include a computer chip (an ASIC) that is able to do the complex calculations needed to find an individual's location on planet earth. Today the Motorola and Samsung smart wrist watches (and others of their ilk) with a mobile cell phone capability combined with a GPS navigation chip represent today's realization of yet another Clarke prophecy come to fruition. As of 2015, some six decades later, his anticipation of the precise, highly portable satellite navigation device is once again right on target. (That is if one can forgive the pun.) Indeed it is amazing that not only are such satellite networks and hand held units now available but that they are also cheap enough—i.e. under $200-- for individuals to buy and use as just a component in a smart phone.

Clarke knew that a network of just three geosynchronous satellites would be just the start to a global navigation satellite network since three Geo birds would constitute only a rudimentary system. His initial vision, however, was for calculating position determination and not designing a mechanism for nuclear war and missile launching and targeting. Unfortunately the original purpose of the U.S. Navstar (i.e. Global Positioning Satellite GPS system) and the Soviet Union's Glonass network was for missile targeting and that it was military objectives and not consumer design that drove the deployment of these satellite networks. Ironically military investment consistently leads to key new applications and systems that the world wants and needs. This very beneficial serendipity is seemingly endemic in our modern world. As Arthur C. Clarke explained in his writings from his adopted home of Sri Lanka that the word "Serendipity" derives from the ancient name of Sri Lanka which was "Serendip"*

---

* The Persian historian Muhammad bin Ahmad in his travels apparently called Sri Lanka "Singal-Dip" This name derived from the Farsi word for island "Sinhala". In the Arabic version of this name it became simply Serendip. This in turn led to the Persian fairy tale known as The Three Princes of Serendip. In this story the protagonists always happened to make inventions or discoveries that they were not seeking. It was on this basis that the English writer Horace Walpole in the 18th century first used the word serendipity to mean unexpected or accidental outcomes of a positive nature.

Today's satellite mobile and navigation satellite technology has actually achieved the ultimate convenience to the world-wide consumer by miniaturization and combining of functions. Today's smart phone combines cellular technology and a GPS chip. Some small but more expensive navigational devices one can buy today, in some cases, also includes a GLANOSS chip that allows access to the other large timing and navigational satellite which is operated by Russia.

By having access to the Navstar (i.e. this is formal name of the GPS network satellites) and also Glasnost satellites one can obtain even greater accuracy. In time it is likely that future generations of smart phones will be able to track multiple timing and navigation satellites. Thus these future devices may include chips and reception capabilities that work not only to Glasnost and GPS but also the European Galileo, the Chinese Beidou and Compass systems, the Indian Regional Navigational System, and perhaps even to the Japanese Quazi-Zenith navigational birds.

These devices because of very smart embedded chips are able to communicate to their various types of satellite networks as well as receive signals at least from the GPS (i.e. Navstar timing and navigational satellites). The technology that makes this possible, namely application specific integrated circuits (ASICs) was not known to Arthur C. Clarke of course. Yet the idea of a miniaturized calculator was anticipated. Today we also have the wristwatch mounted mobile device as noted in the previous chapter. Currently these devices operate only with terrestrial cellular networks, but it is not hard to imagine that in a short period of time these wristwatch devices will be able to link to a satellite phone (or transceiver) that can be carried in a holster or perhaps eventually integrated into one's clothing so that one would only have to interface with the one device.

Today there are also Google glasses that allow one to see wireless transmission of images. Shortly it would seem that these capabilities will be wed together. Thus, the interface device for mobile communications to a satellite, as well as to see a map of where one is currently located and where they are going, could be in time all mounted with a pair of glasses or simply an eye loop and device positioned at the ear that contains a transmitter, receiver and digital signal processor. These would all be quite small. The largest components for connecting to the satellite would be a power supply (small rechargeable battery) and a satellite antenna that might be integrated with one's clothing or discreetly carried in a holster. The designers would simply have to come up with concepts that on one hand would not create a health hazard (by avoiding having RF signaling at an elevated level close to the head and brain) and on the other hand would be virtually invisible. Live wire underwear and brassieres might be the fashion of the next decade. Clearly a navigational aid system that not only told you where you are and how to get there but could also show you in real time exactly what to do anywhere in the world would seem to be a real benefit. This assumes that you could switch such a navigational system on and off at will.

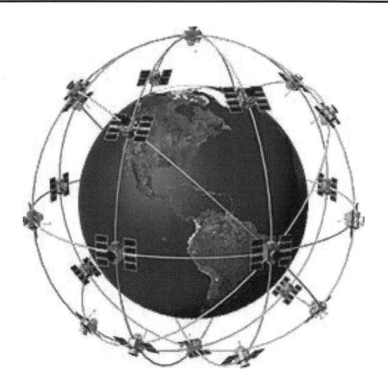

Figure 4.1: The Global Positioning Satellite GPS System

Clarke also anticipated that essentially only one satellite system would be needed for navigation assuming that this system would be global in design and comprehensively available. The GPS system is indeed globally visible and offered at no charge. The current network is shown in Figure 4.1 above.

Clarke's point of departure was that a navigational system might an adjunct to global satellite communications for broadcasting and networking. However, the actual development and deployment of today's timing and navigational satellite networks had a more sinister purpose. The initial systems as deployed by the United States and the Soviet Union were for targeting of bomb laden missiles. In the age of MAD, i.e. mutually assured destruction, space navigation systems were an essential part of national defense and military operations. This was the justification for spending billions of dollars--to be able to destroy cities half way around the world with precision. Today, fortunately we have had no nuclear wars and the use that has been made of these satellites is of a much more practical nature of assisting planes to take off and land, to map and survey, to safely navigate vehicles and ships to their desired location, and to help those who are lost to find their way home.

Conclusions

Today the dreams of Edward Everett Hale and Arthur C. Clarke have not only been realized, but the applications for these "navigators-in-the-sky" have expanded by leaps and bounds. These applications come not only from the satellite's ability to establish precise location, but also to provide time stamps with incredible accuracy. Thus today the precise atomic clock timing of these Precision Navigation and Timing (PNT) satellites provide security systems for time stamping by banks of electronic funds transfer, to coordinate the interaction of the Internet, to provide security authentication for a variety of reasons, and even allow for warnings of dangerous tsunamis. This warning is possible because a slight disruptions in the transmission times through atmospheric transmissions occurs when certain types of earthquakes create.

In terms of application satellite market size, navigation satellites are second only to communications satellites in their direct impact on the global economy. It is estimated that timing and navigation satellites now represent over ten billion dollars in revenues to world economy each year. The real economic impact of these types of satellites can most realistically be considered if these networks were ever to stop operating. The negative impact on the airline, shipping and freight industries, the global banking industry, the E-business carried on the Internet, etc. for a sustained outage would be devastating. The total impact would not be measured in billions of dollars, but potentially in trillions of dollars if the outage lasted for weeks or months.

Chapter 5

Computers and Artificial Intelligence

"Data transmission will bring the skills of giant computers to anyone who needs them. The computers themselves will join forces in a vast network, and automation of industry will become an international reality." **Arthur C. Clarke, _Time_ magazine. Friday 14th April, 1965**

"As the [A.I.] machine improves….we shall begin to see all the phenomena associated with the terms "consciousness", "intuition", and "intelligence" itself…..It is unreasonable to think that machines could become nearly as intelligent as we are and then stop, or to suppose that we will always be able to compete with them in wit and wisdom." **Marvin Minsky, at the time head of the Massachusetts Institute of Technology's artificial intelligence lab (1975).**

"….there is every reason to suppose that machines will become much more intelligent than their builders , as well as incomparably faster.……No individual lasts forever why should we expect our species to be immortal? Man, said Nietzsche, is a rope stretched between the animal [today's human] and the superhuman—a rope across the abyss. That will be a noble purpose to have served." Creating a device that can create copies of itself is something that many scientists have been working towards. Once you pair a self-replicating device with programming to look for improvements, it opens up an interesting door to evolving machines. **Forever Geek.**

"Artificial Intelligence is the most important development of the twentieth century" - **Arthur C. Clarke's response to a question at Comsat Corporation Headquarters, 1970.**

"It can be maintained that every man is perfectly familiar with at least one thinking machine, because he has a late-model sitting on his shoulders. For if the brain is not a machine what is it?" **Arthur C. Clarke, <u>Report on Planet Three and Other Speculations,</u> Signet Books, N.Y. (1973).**

"Assume for the sake of argument that conscious beings have existed for twenty million years: see what strides machines have made in the last thousand!   May not the world last twenty million years longer?   If so, what will they not in the end become." **Samuel Butler, 1871, quoted in Ray Kurzweil's <u>"How to Create a Mind", p274.</u>**

In the Beginning

The concept of a computer, or a machine that is able to make calculations and reason, has been long with us. Johnathan Swift in his book *Gulliver's Travels* wrote in 1726 of a machine that was called simply the Engine that Lemuel Gulliver encounters in the Academy of Projectors in the land of Laganda. This "Engine" is composed of complicated pieces of wood and wires and is able to compose poetry and prose. A century later Charles Babbage developed the Differential Engine (1821-1832) and the Analytical Engine (1856) that became an early prototype of a mechanical calculator and began speculation that some form of computer would be possible. In 1909 E. M. Forster contributed to the literary notion of a computer in his short story "The Machine Stops" wherein technology and computers had become a significant portion of human society and everyday life.

Virtually all of the well-known science fiction writers -- Isaac Asimov, Robert A. Heinlein, Frank Herbert, Fred Hoyle, Stanislaw Lem, and Kurt Vonnegut Jr. to name just a few -- all included interesting and sometimes compelling computers in their stories and novels. Often these sci-fi machines developed not only consciousness but human characteristics and weaknesses as well. In fact many of these "machines" could not only "think" but could also undertake evil plots and agendas that could work against human interests. In this respect Arthur C. Clarke stands out. Certainly, his descriptions of computers and smart machines for the Overlords in *Childhood's End*, for the monks in *The Nine Billion Names of God*, and for the city administrators in Diaspar in *The City and the Stars* were all interesting. But it was the HAL 9000 (for Heuristic Algorithm and not IBM moved forward one letter) that captured worldwide notoriety and fame. In the movie *"2001: A Space Odyssey"* one experienced what seemed to be a living, breathing and ultimately treacherous computer that seemed all too human.

The nature of Clarke's forecasts with regard to computers were severalfold. Each of these will be addressed in turn. Clarke envisioned the following:

- The dramatic increase in computer processing power that would lead to huge reductions in the cost of computer processing.(This is sometimes called the "Rate of Accelerating Returns. This exponential growth of "machine processing" versus the slow rate of biological evolution was what Samuel Butler was driving at in the question he posed in 1871 when he asked what "machines" will be able to achieve in another 1000 years.)
- The result of low-cost, high-speed, broad-band processing—namely a wide range of new applications related to education, health, banking, transportation, power, communications, weather forecasting and entertainment.
- The future breakthroughs in artificial intelligence that will lead to computer-assisted capabilities that equal—and then exceed—human intelligence. Clarke saw this as having not only implications in terms of jobs, employment and future prosperity,

but also having impact on privacy, government, and social intercourse.

- The ultimate achievement of artificial, machine-driven, programmable innovation that leads to the achievement of the VonNeuman machines and rapid artificial evolutionary advances. Clarke has said this could lead to the replacement of humanity at the top of the food chain.

In addition, Arthur C. Clarke also envisioned the Internet and its huge impact on the world from social media, to E-Commerce, to the cloud, but these predictions are addressed elsewhere in the book. The linking of artificial intelligence to global and ultimately galactic networking, however, are addressed in the final analysis in this chapter.

The Greatest 20th Century Invention

In 1970, at a reception held on the eighth floor reception area at Comsat Headquarters in Washington DC, Clarke stunned the crowd when he was asked what he considered to be the greatest invention of the 20th Century. Arthur, with no hesitation, responded "artificial intelligence" and there was an audible gasp around the room. The audience of satellite executives was expecting to hear "satellite communications".

Clarke went on to explain that A.I. would open the doors to a new future for humanity. He explained that communications satellites for instance could be reconfigured to meet new and unexpected needs and accommodate new and more efficient means of encoding. He explained that what was true for communications satellites was true across the board. Artificial intelligences, powered by new generations of quantum supercomputers of tiny proportions would allow dramatic increases in automation and the improvement of services in banking, education, healthcare, energy, retail, transportation, entertainment, and governmental and social services. Even unexpected areas such as farming, police and public safety will benefit from "smart" innovations that make these areas more efficient and responsive to new demands and, of course, unexpected problems like the current bane to society, that of cyber security.

The advances in computer capabilities in terms of processing power have increased at a prodigious rate. The achievable processing speeds are often related to Gordon Moore's Law that predicted the doubling of transistors in integrated circuits (or monolithic devices) every 18 months. Certainly this amazing progress has now proceeded largely unchecked for nearly a half century. Communications systems today are largely digital processing networks that are designed to carry out their function by means of specially crafted "software" specifically defined to meet the goals and functions of electronic connectivity. Thus telecommunications networks closely followed Moore's Law as well.

Few tasks today—whether they involve scientific and engineering work, difficult medical diagnosis, writing and artwork layout for newspapers, magazines and books, farming or investment banking -- are not assisted by computer tools that are becoming smarter and smarter. For years we have called these "expert systems" in that these computer software tools simply morphed together the collective expertise of people in a particular field. As these expert systems become more and more capable the question arises as to when does "artificial intelligence" transcend "expert systems" with a set of algorithms that mimic the thought processes of human experts? The ultimate question is when might machines become "self aware" or perhaps more capable of logic and thought than humans? Samuel Butler was perhaps one of the first to raise this question in a serious way. Arthur C. Clarke seriously thought about smart machines making humans obsolete.

Today, with parallel processing and linked computers, the speeds are truly phenomenal and Petaflops speeds (a thousand trillion calculations a second) are not tied to how many transistors we can place on a chip.. Anyone can now purchase for a few hundred dollars a computer (such as a "smart phone") that is millions of times faster than Univac or any of the earliest computers. It is not speed that limits what computers can and will do. The software part of the puzzle has been by far the hardest. Arthur C. Clarke has said that in the mid-1960s that he had reckoned that a computer the equivalent of "HAL" might have been possible by as early as 1992. However, we seem to be making much more rapid progress today. Some believe that a key turning point was when IBM's "Big Blue" beat Kasparov at chess. Others think that when IBM's "Watson" beat the top champions on the television show Jeopardy that this was a sign of a true turning point. Ray Kurzweil, in his books *The Singularity is Near* and *How to Create a Mind: The Secret of Human Thought Revealed,* explains that we still have good ways to go. Yet he is taking a special regimen of food and drugs with the hope to still be around for another twenty years when the break through to a truly advanced "thinking machine" is achieved.

While philosophers are contemplating the meaning of a thinking machine that is able to create even smarter machines that are self-aware and capable of conscious thought, scientists in laboratories are actually working toward this end. There are several meaningful efforts underway. Professor Henry Markham of France is trying to create the mechanical equivalent of a human brain in terms of a device that can access an equivalent amount of memory in real time and make an equivalent number of logical operations. He has already come quite far in that his "thinking computer" developed in his Blue Brain project. Thus he has already created the real time equivalent of a rat's brain. This translates in to an accessible memory of 5×10^{13} bytes of information and a processing speed of 10^{16} FLOPS. (A flop, or Floating point Operations Per Second, is how computer scientists measure a computer's processing power.)

According to Prof. Markham, a human brain is only a 1000 times more capable in terms of memory and thinking capability (i.e. processing capability). His current goal is to develop by 2023 a human brain equivalent (HBE). Its arithmetic equivalence is something like 5×10^{16} bytes of memory and its processing speed would be 10^{19} FLOPS. (See Ray Kurzweil, *How to Create a Mind,* pp 124-125).

Not everyone agrees that sheer computer firepower is the way to create a fully functional HBE that can be acknowledged as: "IT IS ALIVE!" As

Clarke noted with HAL in "*2001: A Space Odyssey*", it is hard to create a creative Heuristic Algorithm that would simulate the process of "human thinking and emotions". No one truly can define what thinking actually means. But most would agree that a creative artificial intelligence would be able not only to "process" algorithms but somehow be self-aware and capable of undertaking all necessary strategic steps needed to survive in a changing environment. As we saw with HAL, this was a machine that could make moral judgments and devise strategies to survive even if others might suffer as consequence of those decisions.

Scientists at Harvard University are essentially trying to create artificial life on computer systems starting with lower life forms with brains with the equivalent of only 300 neurons and building up from there. These artificial creatures would not only "exist" as simulations but would "evolve" as they existed within a changing environment where they would search for food and ward off enemies. If one wants a scary version of what might happen if one could put a super intelligent human brain online and then allow it to access all the computing power in the world, surf the Internet and multiple clouds and then begin a fight for survival, then one should go see the movie "Transcendence". In this movie the intelligence becomes maniacal and starts building a cyborg army to take over the world.

Hollywood is good at creating "Dystopian" sci-fi thrillers like "Transcendence". But there is at least a reasonable chance that artificial intelligence and HBEs could be designed to provide useful assistance to a future world to help cope with everything from climate change, to the alleviation of poverty, to global cooperation and perhaps especially education and healthcare. At least this is the hope and aspiration of geniuses like Ray Kurdzweil and Henry Markham who are working hard to achieve "thinking machines."

"Smart" Machines and Education

The speech that Arthur made on the occasion of the opening of the new International Programme for the Development of Communications (IPDC) at the UNESCO headquarters in Paris in 1981 suggested to some that certain smart machines would take over a significant role in the future of teaching and play a key part in imparting knowledge around the world--especially where educational systems are lacking. As Clarke succinctly summed it up in an article "Electronics and Education" (which was reprinted later in his collection of speeches and essays in *1984: Spring, A Choice of Futures*): "Every teacher that can be replaced by a machine—should be." When asked by reporters at the UNESCO meeting in Paris: "Was he saying all education could be automated?" Clarke responded: "Of course not". He added, however, that teachers needed to inspire, entice, and motivate and provide key personal contact. If teachers were only doing what a machine could do then they were not doing enough.

In explaining how this new computer explosion in education would take place he noted that this future technology would have more to do with Fisher Price, the toy company, than IBM and high end computer manufacturers. Clarke's "personal tutor" in his vision would be very low cost, pervasively available, even in the developing world, and highly capable of covering any subject and in any language around the world. This particular vision has not yet been achieved, but we are very close. The reason we are not there yet has more to do with business, economic, and cultural reasons than it has to do with technology. Software defined radio technology and low cost mobile communications should allow such a universal "personal tutor" to be available all over the world within a decade or two. Today's manufactures of computer tablets and "smart phones" that sell for several hundreds of dollars probably need to saturate global markets, before Clarke's vision can truly be realized.

The usual thought about artificial intelligence relates to single machines. In the case of IBM's "Watson" there are a number of processors with a great deal of information that is rather instantly accessible. With today's computer networks, however, an artificial intelligence can be linked around the world and into outer space. The issue that artificial intelligence poses for humanity thus becomes not only how "smart" can it become, but how pervasive does it become in our lives? The U.S. National Security Agency is creating a data storage facility in a remote part of Utah that will literally be able to store Yottabytes of information. (This number, named after Yoda from Star Wars represents a quadrillion gigabits). Some feel that such a massive information storage capability will spell the end to human privacy. Once artificial intelligence capabilities are developed in terms of software it can be distributed worldwide and replicated in hundreds of locations and stored within the cloud. The future is thus increasingly looking like ever smarter algorithms that are widely distributed on global networks and stored in the cloud and linked to unlimited amounts of memory. This suggests the ability to unlock huge intellectual resources to cope with the world's problems, but it also suggests the end of privacy.

This evolving future of super networked intelligence is, of course, vividly portended in one of Arthur C. Clarke's most well-known science fiction books *Childhood's End*. In this book the Overlords come to await this epochal event. In this particular story, all human young people create a massive mind meld to form a massive global brain of unified super intelligence. It was never clear what the message of this seminal book was meant to be. It might, in fact, have been not only a prediction of what could happen, not in a biological sense, but in terms of linked computer memory and global shared artificial intelligence algorithms. We, as humanity, need to consider what the consequences of such a transformation might be regardless of whether such a massive mind-meld came from a natural biological evolution or from a global artificially-intelligent network with incredible memory and processing speeds.

In the U.S.-based television show "A Person of Interest", such a pervasive artificially-intelligent machine exists. This machine indeed has access to all electronic networks to talk to people, spy on them, and to control their actions. Although the intent of such a machine, with its super processing powers, was initially intended as a good, the potential for oppressive misuse has become a constant theme of the television series. In the 1950s when *Childhood's End* was written the story seemed entertaining yet far removed from reality. Today this classic Arthur C. Clarke story appears as yet another apocryphal warning of a future that might be created through networked machine artificial intelligence.

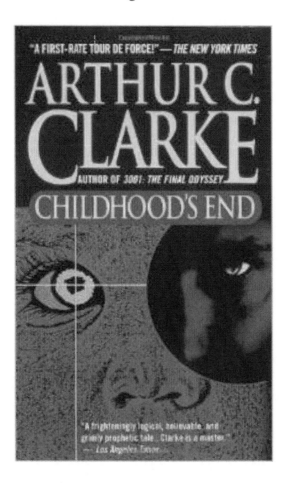

Figure 5.1: Clarke's <u>*Childhood's End*</u> *Foretold of a World Dominated by All Young Humans Who Could Think Together with One Merged Global Brain.*

Conclusions

Today we may be nearing the limits of what can be achieved in terms of transistors etched in solid state materials to create monolithic integrated circuit devices. This is due to natural radioactive decay that eventually changes the device's functionality. Quantum computers appear to be the next threshold of what raw processing power can be achieved. Today there is talk not of hand-held computers, but of computers the size of blood cells with enormous processing power. A computer that operated at exaflop speeds would indeed need to be of very tiny size to overcome the limitation of the speed of light.

The limits of the future are perhaps not be found in teraflop, petaflop, exaflop, or even zettaflop or yottaflops processing speeds, but rather in the limits to software developed for creating artificial intelligence, truly functional heuristic algorithms and "machine reasoning" capabilities. Today's expert systems can match doctors' ability to diagnose illnesses, and give CPA's a run for their money in putting together tax returns. Clearly we have merely touched the surface of what might yet be when the "Singularity" occurs. When that day arrives, we will indeed have computers armed with AI that exceed human capabilities. Clearly we are still a few years away from a machine like Arthur C. Clarke's HAL, but we may find that Prof. Henry Markham's estimate of 2023 might not be too far off the mark of a time when we start to produce at least a few very smart and 'thinking' machines indeed.

We will return to the limits of heuristic algorithms in Chapter 13 in Part II when we explore predictions yet to be realized.

Chapter 6

Energy and Power

"Our goal should be to achieve clean, safe, and cheap sources of energy that are available to all those who need it, wherever they need it. Options such as solar, wind and biomass have been proven, while other methods, such as Ocean Thermal Conversion (OTEC) are less widely known and tested". **Arthur C. Clarke, "Our Guide to the Future" Business Today, May 2008.**

"For one thing, there is this so-called cold fusion. Which is neither cold nor fusion. Very few Americans seem to know what is happening, which is incredible. It's all over the world, except the United States. There are hundreds of laboratories doing it, they've got patents all over the place. The prototypes are on sale now …. There are so many vested interest. There are the hot fusion boys. All the rocket engineers will be out of jobs, and a lot of the poor guys are already. I don't like to guess at the scenario, but I would say that before the end of this decade, the hand waving will be over and people will accept that this energy exists, whatever it is, and there may actually be several different varieties. A lot of heads will roll at the U.S. Department of Energy and elsewhere."- **an excerpt from Arthur C.Clarke's Comments to Discover Magazine, May 1997.**

"…fossil fuels such as coal and oil can last for only a few more centuries; then they will be gone forever. They will have served to launch our technological culture into its trajectory, by providing easily available sources of energy, but they

cannot sustain civilization over thousands of years. For this we need something more permanent." **Arthur C. Clarke, "Profiles of the Future"** *, Guernsey Press, GB (1988).*

"...fission is the dirtiest and most unpleasant method of releasing energy that man has ever discovered......But beyond fission lies fusion—the welding together of light atoms such as hydron and lithium. This is the reaction that drives the stars themselves; we have reproduced it on Earth, but have not yet tamed it. When we have done so our power problems will have been solved forever." **"Ages of Plenty",** *Arthur C. Clarke,* **"Profiles of the Future"** *Guernsey, Press, GB (1988).*

"OTEC is the answer to OPEC" - **Arthur C. Clarke's mantra**

One of the amazing facets of Arthur C. Clarke's brain is how he constantly fed it new and important data. When I visited his spacious, almost vast office that was the main room on the upper floor at Barnes Place, I was struck with its library of current journals that cover not just space and astronautics, but every field from oceanography to telecommunications, from computers to energy. He had a passion to consume as much facts and scientific and artistic and cultural information as possible. Power and energy was one of his many favorite subjects. He realized that everything that existed everywhere was composed of matter, energy, and time. He thus knew instinctively that he needed to know as much as possible about each. He knew that Earth held an infinitesimal amount of the cosmos' mass and energy and that ultimately, humans would need to leave our tiny cradle to achieve anything of truly cosmic importance.

Clarke's approach in his predictions to energy and power harken back to his three laws. He analyzed that which was currently available but was insufficient—in terms of long term supply and environmental sustainability, and then sought to push the boundaries into the unknown as to what might be converted from today's impossibility or assumed magic into a future reality.

Let us go back to Clarke's review of technology that is divided into the "unexpected" and the "expected" (in chapter 1). It is just assumed (i.e. expected) that someday a clever person will find unlimited and clean energy that is available to everyone. The source of the power is likely to unexpected. As Clarke has observed, nuclear fusion is perhaps the most likely source, but there may well be ways to tap into cosmic energy, create new ways to capture and use solar power, and so on.

Certainly solar has much to commend it. In terms of longevity the Sun will be a reliable source of energy as long as there is a habitable Earth. The source is indeed free and does not have to be dug up or liberated. And according to Arthur's own calculations the solar nuclear reactor produces some 500,000,000,000,000,000,000.000 horsepower on a rather continuous basis. Even though recent solar observations have shown that there is about a 1% variation in the power generated. Ray Kurzweil has helpfully observed that the Sun sends 10,000 times more energy to Earth that human's currently use. The problem that Arthur C. Clarke noted was that the Sun's power is spread out over the Solar System much like an omni (or isotropic) antenna, with a gain that is typically close to 1 except for occasional narrowly focused coronal mass ejections and solar flares. And for the solar energy that does reach Earth the magnetosphere and the Van Allen belts diverts a good deal of it and then the atmosphere absorbs a lot of the energy as well. Thus what we end up with at sea level is about one horsepower per square yard. Since today's solar cells are only about 20% efficient that is certainly not very useful for direct application to transport. In his analysis Clarke also largely discounted gravity and the Earth's natural electro-magnetic field as a viable source of power.

Certainly things are improving in the solar power arena. Ultraviolet solar cells with multiple junctions and gallium arsenide composition can produce over 40% efficiencies, but these are currently expensive. Quantum dot technology, now in the labs, will boost conversion efficiencies even further, but the bottom line is that solar energy is currently better suited to thermal control systems for buildings and housing than it is for powering transportation systems. Clearly solar power systems of the future that provide the electrical power to charge batteries and fuel cells could certainly work. They could even provide the power for generators to produce compressed air that could power cars as well.

Arthur C. Clarke, however, largely looked beyond solar power to examine the power that can come from the atom. In his predictions and forecasts, he essentially had a view of nuclear fission as a power source that lay somewhere between distain and complete contempt and derision. His statement: "fission is the dirtiest and most unpleasant method of releasing energy that man has ever discovered" pretty much sums up his views on the subject. He notes that nuclear waste will still be creating severe radiation dangers thousands of years after they have been created. It is too bad that Clarke is not around to testify at hearings where atomic power is extolled as an environmentally friendly way to produce power that is much better than coal-fired plants. This is a true case of the pot calling the kettle black. Coal and nuclear-fission are clearly power technologies of the past and he understood this thoroughly. The potential of nuclear fusion was where Arthur gave very high marks. He foresaw this technology as being much more highly efficient, clean, and in time perhaps very cost efficient.

It was thus on nuclear fusion that he felt research should be concentrated. He admonished us to give focus to "taming" nuclear fusion—the process that powers the stars themselves. And when this feat is accomplished then all would be well, in Clarke's view: *When we have done so [i.e. tamed nuclear fusion] our power problems will have been solved forever.*" Part of his special gift is that he always tempered his visionary genius with a clear scientific and engineering understanding of where technology advances were possible in reasonable periods of time. He had seen promises to achieve nuclear fusion come and go over many decades and remained skeptical that the taming of this process was on our doorstep. Thus he examined other intermediary sources of energy in the nearer term.

One of Clarke's favorite "clean and renewable" energy sources was from Ocean Terminal Energy Conversion (OTEC). Every time we discussed energy, his mantra came forth *"OTEC is the answer to OPEC"*. Of course OTEC is, in essence yet another form of solar energy that can be employed to make liquid hydrogen as a fuel. In a OTEC plant such as the Mitsubishi plant off the shore of the big island of Hawaii the process works this way. Solar concentrators focus energy on the water's surface to heat it to high temperatures. Then the heat differential between the hot water at the surface and the cold at the lower depths are used , in effect, to run a "turbine" or a "heat exchange" process to produce energy in a series of cycles. This can be used to achieve water desalinization, to generate electricity or create a fuel such as liquid hydrogen from the ocean water.

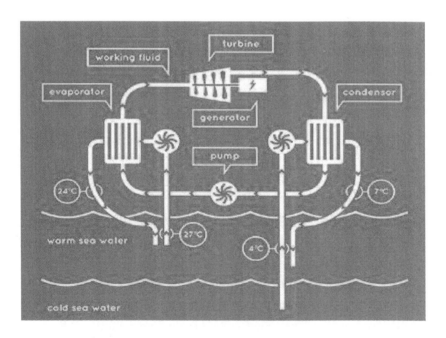

Figure 6.1: The Basic Principles of OTEC Energy Generation

Figure 6.1 above shows the basic principles of OTEC operations. The use of solar concentrators to heat the water can make the process more efficient. Also there can be a design that takes advantage of multiple heat-to-cold water cycles. So far the technology has not been developed to a state where the energy production is sufficiently cost effective to compete with other conventional energy sources but just like solar, the time will come when both these technologies will be cheaper than coal. If one adds in the cost of cleaning up after coal pollution, that time is now.Clarke recognized that essentially there were two forms of energy. The energy we use is created either by human extraction, burning or turbine processes (such as burning coal, oil and gas, hydro-electric and wind turbines or nuclear reactors) or cosmic energy (i.e. soaking up solar energy directly) In the case of solar or cosmic energy the sources comes from mass conversion (i.e. fusion) or gravitational and magnetic effects (solar flares and coronal mass ejections). Most of the energy that we use on Earth today has at one time or another come from the Sun. Oil and coal and other forms of chemical energy are just stored energy that once came from the Sun. Further Clarke has noted that our reservoirs of oil and coal and other hydrocarbon fuel sources are rapidly being used up with only a few centuries to go. Wind and tidal energy essentially also come from the Sun and the Moon, but fortunately this is a replenishable energy source.

In short—not to put too fine a point on it--Clarke diagnosed that our planet is running out of gas. His conclusion was a very simple and direct one. We will rely on the remaining hydrocarbon fuels and after that on the other renewables such as solar, wind, OTEC and tidal generators until we ultimately find a way to emulate the star's own methods of generating energy. If we ultimately succeed in this we will have limitless clean energy. Currently we are beginning to wean ourselves off of hydrocarbon and transitioning to recyclable green fuels. The ultimate transition to nuclear fusion that we will use to power human civilization here on Earth and to create starships to leave the Earth's gravity well—i.e. the third plateau of human's energy history -- is still perhaps decades away. This is a case where we cannot say that Arthur C. Clarke's forecasts were wrong, but that human history has not yet caught up to his prophecy. As we will learn in the later chapters, however, new "compact fusion", which now appears to be on the horizon, may bring this prediction to fruition faster than we thought just a year ago.

In some ways we already seem to be tantalizingly close to achieving Clarke's prediction of limitless clean energy from nuclear fusion, yet still very far away. Figure 6.2 below shows a fusion plasma apparatus at the U.S. National Sandia Labs that in September 2012 achieved some 500 terawatts of power output. But this was only a one time and tiny instant "shot" event. Such a one time achievement in a special lab experiment suggests we are still some time away from Clarke's vision of the ultimate answer to humanity's growing appetite for electrical power.

*Figure 6.2: Plasma Container where a 500 Terawatt Fusion Event Occurred in 2012
(Graphic Courtesy of Sandia)*

The concept, variously known as Chemically Assisted Nuclear Reaction, Low Energy Nuclear Reaction, Muon catalyzed fusion, sono luminensce, desktop fusion and cold fusion, thoroughly captured Clarke's imagination the decade before his death.

In the late 1980s, Martin Fleischmann a leading electrochemist and Stanley Pons at the University of Utah experimented with palladium and electrolytic mixtures and came up with some very peculiar results of unexplained amounts of heat energy. They announced the discovery in March 1989 and set off a debate about the feasibility of desktop or "cold fusion" that continues to this day.

The unexplained heat release occurs under certain conditions in metal hydrides (metals with hydrogen or heavy hydrogen dissolved in them). The result is a release of heat and helium. The allegation is that the helium comes from "fused" hydrogen atoms. The experiments also have claimed to produce charged particles, and occasionally a very low level of neutrons and even tritium. Experimenters continue to work in this field although many nuclear physicists disparage the idea of "room temperature" fusion events stimulated by electrochemical processes.

Clarke died still hoping that some chemically induced nuclear fusion events might be possible. As always he was open-minded enough to find hope in a totally new and unexpected idea. Thus he found the possibility of a new clean power source as an appealing idea that he explored with gusto in the 1990s and 2000s with the hope that it could eventually prove to be more than a quirky idea. For the time being we will simply have to wait and see as research continues under the banner of Chemically Assisted Nuclear Reactions and Low Energy Nuclear Reactions.

Conclusions

Arthur C. Clarke spent a good part of his later years contemplating the issue of worldwide dependence on hydrocarbon fuels. He felt over dependence on oil was one of humanity's bigger mistakes. He considered renewable, green energy as a better source of power than air-polluting coal and oil. He also felt that the "power of the sun", namely nuclear fusion, was the longer terms answer both on and off the planet. In part this conclusion derived from his vision that humans must ultimately travel to other star systems and here only nuclear fusion could work. Solar sails might work within the solar system, but not beyond. He also recognized the beauty of nuclear fusion so elegantly and beautifully revealed in Einstein's equation $E = MC^2$. The elegance of this equation was to him like a godlike signal or signpost to the future for all of humanity's energy needs.

As the world waits to develop the key technology needed to harness the power released from nuclear fusion, Clarke also embraced the idea of using green and renewable energy, from photo electric cells (i.e. solar cells) to ocean thermal energy conversion, to tidal energy systems, to wind turbines and more. His hope was that low energy nuclear reaction was one short cut to the future, but so far this has not been the case.

On his 90th birthday, not long before his death in 2008, Arthur C. Clarke provided us with his three wishes for humanity. These were:

"1. Evidence of extraterrestrial life....E.T. call us."

"2. Cleaner energy sources for the future of civilization, here and beyond Earth."

"3. Lasting peace, both in my adopted Sri Lanka and in the world."

Unfortunately humanity still seems far from being able to delivering on any one of these three wishes.

Chapter 7

Robots, Cyborgs and Bio–Engineering

"...the Committee on Biological Engineering and advanced Robotics proposed that future transfers be accomplished using suspended zygotes together with new versions of the super-intelligent robots serving as zoo monitors". **Arthur C. Clarke and Gentry Lee, Cradle (1988).**

"What Nature can do, Man can do also, in his own way. In the end we learned to analyse and store the information that would define any specific human being—and to use that information to recreate the original." **Arthur C. Clarke, The City and the Stars (1956).**

"One can imagine a time when men who still inhabit organic bodies are regarded with pity by those who have passed on to an infinitely richer mode of existence, capable of throwing their consciousness or sphere of attention instantaneously to any point on land, sea, or sky where there is a suitable sensing organ. In adolescence we leave childhood behind; one day there may be a second and more portentous adolescence, when we bid farewell to the flesh." **Arthur C. Clarke, Profiles of the Future Guernsey Press, Great Britain (1988).**

"It is too late to worry about if computers will take over the world. Let us hope that our silicon successors will treat us kindly." **Arthur C. Clarke Interview with Representatives from the Internet Society in Sri Lanka, April 2002.**

"Our bodies are not like machines, they never wear out, because they are continually rebuilt from new materials. If this process were uniformly efficient, we would be immortal. Unfortunately, after a few decades something goes wrong to the repair-and-maintenance department; the materials are as good as ever, but the old plans get lost or ignored, and vital services are not property restored when they break down. It is as if the cells of the body can no longer remember the jobs they once did so well." **Arthur C. Clarke, _Profiles of the Future,_ Guernsey Press, Great Britain (1988).**

"In some form or other, the idea of artificial intelligence goes back at least three thousand years. Before he turned his attention to aeronautical engineering, Daedalus—King Minos' one man Office of Scientific Research constructed a metal man to guard the Coast of Crete." **Arthur C. Clarke, _Report on Planet Three and Other Speculations,_ Signet Books, NY (1973).**

"The body is the vehicle of the brain, and the brain is the seat of the mind…..If we cannot prevent our bodies from disintegrating, we may replace them while there is time…The replacement need not be another body of flesh and blood, it could be a machine, and this may represent the next stage in evolution. Even if the brain is not immortal, it could certainly live much longer than the body whose diseases and accidents eventually bring it low." **Arthur C. Clarke, _Profiles of the Future_ Guernsey Press, Great Britain (1988).**

The idea of a robot that mimics human capability has been with us for a long, long time, although the specific term 'robot' only dates back to Capek's play R.U.R. (Rossum's Universal Robots) written in 1920. The idea of a mechanical device that could carry out humanlike activities dates back to the time of ancient Crete in the days of King Minos where in myth "metal men" patrolled the coast against invaders. Also a three legged walking table is described in Chapter 37 in the Book of Ezekiel in the Bible. Clearly it was not Arthur C. Clarke who made the first prediction with regard to robots and how they might perform various tasks and develop new human like capabilities.

Robots as a modern literary conception, that include the idea of a mobile humanoid machine, well equipped with an advanced artificial intelligence, are more fairly recent ideas. Cybernetic organisms, also known as "cyborgs", which involve the idea of artificially grown bio organisms with intelligence or computers containing artificial intelligence are even more recent. Today there are a number of somewhat similar yet differentiated concepts known as androids, cyborgs, replicants and robots.

The images of robotic-like devices have covered a very wide range of possibilities. These have varied from the amusing images that have appeared in films such as the endearing Wall-e, the R2D2 and C3P0 robotic team in the Star Wars series, the always smiling servant robots in Woody Allen's "Sleeper", and the totally inept robotic devices depicted in Brazil. These robots were non-threatening and generally depicted as willing helpmates.
There have been various cyborg organisms such as the 'Cybermen 'created for the Dr. Who television series and 'Data' on the Star Trek series. The concept of a "replicant" was depicted in the film "Blade Runner" with these bio-engineered cybernetic organisms being smarter and more attractive than humans.

Today many believe that cloning and bio-engineering may lead to highly capable androids before we can create mechanical robots with comparable intelligence and athletic capabilities. Certainly we today seem very much on the cusp of such capabilities as implanting computer chips into human bodies to supplement our memory systems in order to enhance our ability to recall essential information as an adjunct to our brains. What is less clear is how close are we to totally decoding the human genome in a way that we can engineer humans that are smarter, can live longer, and can be more physically and sexually attractive?

And in an even more worrisome context in future years we might even bio-engineer 'bio-slaves' who are designed to be subservient and to take orders. Arthur C. Clarke, in Profiles of the Future, notes that it might well be possible to go beyond the imaginative world of George Orwell's 1984 and envision a world in which human thoughts could control the thoughts and actions of a bio-slave. Clarke noted research where monkeys had pressed buttons several times a second for 18 hours without stopping (even when enticed by food or sex) in order to fire electrodes that stimulated the pleasure center of their brain. He suggested that this approach could be used to take "electronic possession of human robots".

The Arrival of HAL in "2001 - a Space Odyssey"

Certainly we have already encountered in the world of science fiction some very sinister futuristic profiles of this nature. The idea of ape-like creatures with embedded chips and electronic controls that are given menial tasks has shown us the possible dark side of humanoid bio-engineering and "electronic possession of brains", whether these be monkeys or humans. The vision of how humans might one day interact with artificially intelligent robotic systems that is perhaps most deeply etched in our minds was definitely given to us by Arthur C. Clarke with HAL 9000 that was essentially the controller of the spaceship in the movie "2001: A Space Odyssey".

There are at least two reasons why the image of HAL is quite so vivid a half century after the film "2001" was first shown. First Stanley Kubrick was a masterful director who knew how to make compelling movies and create powerful and unforgettable images. But second, we can credit

Arthur with his own efforts to create the intellectual image of an artificially intelligent HAL in a way that was as sophistically accurate and believable as possible. The characterization of HAL, and indeed his very name, derived from MIT guru Dr. Marvin Minsky, who many considered to be the world's leading researcher on artificial intelligence—at least as of the 1960s when the film was made. The very name HAL was chosen to reflect the idea of **H**euristic **Al**gorithms—or the exact analog of human thought processes. HAL was not conceived to be just a machine with circuits and components, but an artificial entity that could reason, learn, feel, and even be human enough to conspire against the crew to achieve self-survival. We all "expect" mechanical robots to be able to solve logical or mathematical problems, but the most disturbing aspect of the personification of HAL 9000 was the depiction in the film of a 'thinking entity' capable of engaging in conspiracy.

Science fiction writers had previously conceived of robots and artificial intelligence that might be evil. But Clarke and Kubrick created HAL who could engage in deceit, manipulative actions and even deadly conspiracy. It was these very human treacheries that made HAL so memorable.

But Clarke envisioned more than a future populated with robots that were helpers or antagonists. He foresaw a future where humans became one with their machines in the pursuit of greatly extended life. These machines could of course be robotic metallic/plastic/rubber structures or they could be some form of bio-engineered entity.

What Next? *Homo Electronicus?*

And Clarke's speculation also went beyond bio-engineering and prosthetics to extend human lives or just to make us smarter. He explored a rich new range of possibilities. He envisioned a world in which humans evolved to become something beyond *homo sapiens.* In *Childhood's End* a monumental breakthrough creates a new humanity that was a totally linked together in a world mind meld. In this same book Clarke also envisions the development and use of birth control pills and DNA testing.

These developments now seem commonplace. But just try to imagine a world where humans can communicate with each other simply by transmitting Alpha and Beta waves from our brains. Would this be the start of *homo electronicus?*

In many of Clarke's writing, he muses about evolutionary processes that always create higher and improved life forms and asks the profound question of why should *homo sapiens* be different? In my own writings in *e-Sphere: The Rise of the World Wide Mind* I discussed the very real possibility of the evolution of a smarter and more capable intelligent being, *Homo Electronicus.* Today about 10% to 11% of the population of the most developed countries are represented by so-called "digital natives" who have only lived in a completely digital world with broadband mobile communications. Who knows what will happen when several generations of humans are nothing but digital natives?

Today there is a wide range of robots actually in production. These robots are being   designed to carry out tasks large and small. A number of these robots are quite logically being designed to carry out tasks too dangerous for people. Thus there are robots that handle toxic chemicals, bacteriological agents and nuclear materials because these are too dangerous for humans to come into contact with, even for short periods of time.

There are other robotic devices such as a swarm of sensors that can be used to detect enemy combatants and explosive devices. There are also unmanned autonomous vehicles (UAVs) that provide aerial surveillance and even attack missiles and weaponry.

***Figure 7.1: Marilyn Monroe Robot Developed to Walk
and Communicate
(Image Courtesy of Japanese Ministry of International Trade and
Industry)***

Today's remotely controlled UAVs armed with rockets are not too far removed from Clarke's idea of electronic human robot soldiers. Then there are more mundane devices such as robotic vacuum sweepers, floor waxers, and toys. These devices, however, are becoming more and more sophisticated and are capable of more and more functions. A number of projects in locations around the world have created full scale-models of a Marilyn Monroe robot (Figure 7.1 above) but in this case the industrial applications are not yet clear.

As one looks to the future, intelligent robots or android devices seem to be an almost inevitable development in the next decade or two. Already we have a growing number of robots with some degree of intelligence that are available to sweep our floors, or even park and drive our cars. Who knows what "smart products" Google© currently has under development in its labs?

The use of bio-engineered cybernetic organisms or advanced robots with artificial intelligence for space exploration--and even lunar or Martian settlements--are clear-cut concepts that are being developed seriously by space agencies like NASA and ESA. The rover devices deployed on Mars have the ability to move on command and carry out a number of complex chemical tests and experiments. Currently Carnegie Mellon is working with NASA to develop a new generation of Lunar Rovers that are completely remotely controlled.

Figure 7.2:   Robotically Controlled Lunar Rover
(graphic courtesy of NASA)

The Lunar XPrize has over a dozen entries trying to send robotic devices to the Moon to provide live video coverage of various sites, including the original Apollo 11 landing site. Many of the latest versions of fighter jets and bombers are being designed to be pilotless, while surveillance drones are increasingly being designed to be more and more autonomous.

If ever there were to be a permanent lunar colony or a Mars settlement, the early stages would likely be carried out by cyborgs or robots that would not be subject to radiation sickness or have a problem with a lack of oxygen to breathe. These mobile workers might be remotely controlled by humans, but in the time frame that such space colonies might be established they would likely have artificial intelligence close to or perhaps exceeding that of at least the average human IQ. Artificial intelligence expert Ray Kurzweil has projected that the "Singularity" of mobile machines with human-like intelligence will come to be available with the next two decades. As noted earlier, Professor Henry Markham who has created rat brain equivalence expects to achieve human brain equivalence within the next decade. The precise projection is 2023.

The real advantage of robotic devices in a space colony equipped with robotic devices capable of mining and other tasks is that it might well be possible to create a factory that could—with the proper raw material resources at hand -- produce a new generation of robots. In time these factories might be inhabited by humans or could, for instance, produce application satellites that could be lowered into Earth orbit at a fraction of the cost of launching them from the Earth's surface. Such communications, remote sensing, or navigation satellites could be "lowered" using low cost electronic ion propulsion to geosynchronous orbit (or other orbits) on a much lower energy budget than today's chemical rockets. The graphic below shows such a concept -- a fully automated lunar manufacturing colony, as conceived by a NASA study. Perhaps such a capability is only a couple or three decades away.

The idea of a self-growing robotic factory brings us close to the concept provided in Arthur C. Clarke's *2010: Odyssey Two.* This is the idea of the deployment of von Neumann machines in space which are artificially intelligent. Here again, Clarke was a perhaps only a few decades ahead of reality.

The basic idea of a von Neumann machine is not only that it can completely "self-grow" itself but in the replication process also possibly make improvements in its original design. This concept will be discussed later in chapters on the future.

In the case of *2010: Odyssey Two,* a rapidly growing number of von Neumann machines were deployed in space. These von Neumann machines replicated themselves with the mission to compress the gases of Jupiter in such a way as to turn this giant planet into a new mini-star dubbed Lucifer. This surprising new development was to support the development of intelligent life on Jupiter's satellite Europa which has frozen lakes of water, but with sentient creatures living in the waters below this icy surface.

Conclusions

Arthur C. Clarke not only envisioned the design and manufacture of artificially sentient creatures, but the possibility that they would become a part of the world's economic system and would play an important role in the world of the future here on Earth and in space. Today there are driverless cars and fighter jets, "smart utilities" that can be programmed to do our washing, etch a monolithic chip to molecular precision, manufacture the next generation of laptop computer, or produce a shiny new Tesla© sports car. Clarke did not make specific predictions as to the exact date when we would see driverless cars or drone space ships, but he did see the inevitability of artificial intelligence and "thinking" robots and von Neumann machines that would perform more and more tasks in 21st century society. He, like Isaac Asimov, and other science fiction writers saw that humans and thinking machines would live in a symbiotic relationship in the future. It was his hope that these increasingly smart machines would "be kind" to the slow witted humans with which they shared their existence. As humans face extreme challenges in coming decades, such as the weakening of the Earth's magnetosphere, changes to the Van Allen belts, or "climate disruption", it may be these smart machines that provide the technology and the intelligence to allow humanity to survive. Clarke, on balance, felt that artificial intelligence in the longer term was the hope for humanity rather than the source of its demise as some dystopian science fiction writers have suggested. Let's hope that once again he was right.

Chapter 8

The Internet, E–Mail, and Wikipedia

"Data transmission will bring the skills of giant computers to anyone who needs them. The computers themselves will join forces in a vast network, and automation of industry will become an international reality." **Arthur C. Clarke, Time Magazine article,1965.**

"A World Information Center will catalogue and make available the expanding mass of information now threatening to swamp the world's libraries. With easy access to the center by satellite-relayed phone calls from any spot on earth and with computers programmed to do their tedious reference hunting for them, researchers will save countless man-hours as they make use of all the recorded knowledge of the human race." **Arthur C. Clarke, Time Magazine article, 1965.**

"In 2001 every household will have a computer and be connected all over the world. You will be able to purchase tickets and everything that you need to carry on your life." **Arthur C. Clarke Interview by Australian Broadcasting Corporation, 1974.**

"Networks that provides information to the world in real time without censorship will prevent atrocities and even governmental crimes against humanities." **Arthur C. Clarke, Report from Planet Three and Other Speculations (1972).**

Arthur C. Clarke, some fifty years ago in his cover story for *Time* magazine, clearly anticipated not only the Internet, but also texting, e-mail and communication systems such as the World Wide Web. This has led to the rise of phenomena such as Wikipedia, e-magazines and journals, e-tail sales, online porn, and a host of other electronic phenomena—both positive and negative. Clarke foresaw all these developments with astonishing accuracy.

Actually, the first elements of Clarke's prediction of the rise of the Internet came before 1965. The Internet, like many innovations, came in the wake of the Sputnik launch and the perceived "missile gap" in the U.S. In this new space age environment the U.S. Defense Department (DOD) decided that it was necessary to link its major space defense systems in Colorado and Nebraska with the Pentagon to speed decisions, including the possible launch of nuclear weapons. DOD tasked the Defense Advanced Research Projects Agency (DARPA) to accomplish this task. M.I.T. Professor Joseph Licklider was called upon to head the team to devise what became the Advanced Research Project Agency Network, or simply ARPANET. The men who actually developed the packet switched network and the Transmission Code Protocol/Internet Protocol included Larry Roberts, Vint Cerf and Robert Kahn. They had considerable support from M.I.T. faculty and staff.

The unique design of the packet switched network was based on small packets of data that could be routed along multiple pathways, but with the routing address in the "header" of the packet. This would allow all the packets to eventually get to their intended destination and to be reassembled via a multi-node network that in the minds of the designers would benefit from such de-centralized routing. The innovative design was optimized for resilience so that the more pathways and networks that were added to the network of networks the more resistant it would be against possible interruption—or nuclear attack. Today tens of thousands of intranets combine to form the many, many data networks around the world that makes this global network of networks very resilient to interruption. The Internet today is truly not a network, but a kluge of systems networked together with amazing efficiency and resilience. Senator Al Gore was the object of derision when he ran for President for his claim to have started the Internet. But, in fact, from his position in the U.S. Senate he was definitively a key advocate and supporter of new information technology and he strongly backed the growth and development of the Internet. He was, among other things, a prime force behind the Congressional Office of Technology Assessment. In 1975 I was on a panel in Washington, D.C. at the World Future Society Congress with then Senator Gore and Congressman Rose. The topic of discussion was the future of space and terrestrial communications networks. It was clear at that time that he was indeed one of the key backers in Congress of this new digital technology in all its forms.

Indeed my first exposure to ARPANET was in in the late 1970s and early 1980s when I was at Intelsat and working a good deal with Professor Ithiel de Sola Pool of M.I.T. and Richard Solomon of the M.I.T. Media Lab. They used ARPANET for all of their computer communications. To them e-mail was already an everyday reality. But around the world personal computers and common usage of e-mail were still far into the future. In the 1980s personal computers started to come on the scene in a big way. But it was only when the World Wide Web was invented that the Internet as well as e-mail took off.

An English computer scientist named Timothy Berners-Lee was tasked with creating an efficient way to share information among researchers at what was then known as CERN (now known as the European Center on Particle Physics Research). This way of sharing information and data bases among web sites became instantly popular among universities around the world and the Internet spread like gangbusters in the 1990s.

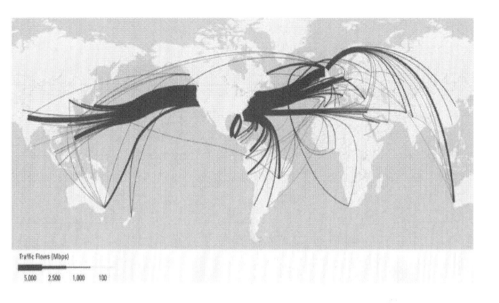

Traffic Flows (Mbps)

5,000 2,500 1,000 100

Figure 8.1: Global Data Flows Via the Internet
(Graphic Courtesy of the Internet Society)

Today the vast flow of information via the Internet is phenomenal as shown in the global data flow map for Internet above. The fact that there is actually ten times more data that flows through corporate and private intranets and so-called "enterprise networks" is more staggering stillThe part of Clarke's prediction about individuals having widely distributed and easy access to giant computers (what we today call super computers) has been the most recent development. Today people in companies, universities and governmental agencies all over the world are storing information and using computer power from the so-called "cloud" without really understanding exactly what this rather vague computer resource actually entails. The U.S. National Institute of Standards and Technology (NIST) has defined the key elements of cloud computing to include: (i) ubiquitous and convenient access; and (ii) on-demand access to an expandable pool of computer processing power and storage. Figure 8.2 below provides a more in-depth understanding of what cloud computing systems actually entail.

It was Clarke's remarkable vision to foresee that all of the accumulated information in the world could essentially be combined on webpages and be accessible via the World Wide Web. He has said in an interview with the Internet Society that Timothy Berners-Lee, the person who first devised the WWW system, had once confessed to him that it was in reading Clarke's *Dial F for Frankenstein* that he first began thinking about how he might create the information display system that now dominates the display of all electronic information. With this disclosure Arthur C. Clarke chuckled and said "I guess that also makes me the Godfather of the Web".

It was equally prescient of Clarke to envision the advent of cloud computing so that 'giant computers' would be available to 'anyone who needs them'. The idea that something like the Internet could allow remote access to broadband networks (via terrestrial, satellite and mobile telecommunications and IT systems) all over the world is perhaps the most remarkable idea of all.

Yet Clarke did go beyond just the technical concepts of advanced communications and information technology systems to consider what might be the implications of such powerful new instruments in terms of privacy, freedom and liberty, and future modes of warfare and political power. On one hand he felt that ubiquitous coverage of human activity via global telecommunications, broadcasting and computer networks would make the conduct of warfare and naked aggression much more difficult to pursue. Systematic studies of aggression carried out around the world since World War II have consistently noted that the incidence has decreased compared with earlier years. Certainly naked aggression, rape, genocide and so-called "crimes against humanity" were much easier to undertake prior to the middle of the Twentieth Century than today where network television cameras, smart phones with cameras, and mobile devices are almost ubiquitous in the developed and increasingly so in the developing world. Tyranny exposed is much more difficult than tyranny under wraps.

KEY CHARACTERISTICS OF CLOUD COMPUTING

On-demand self-service. A consumer can unilaterally provision the use of computing capabilities, such as server time and network storage, as needed automatically without requiring human interaction with each service provider.

Broad network access. Capabilities are available over the network and accessed through standard mechanisms that promote use by heterogeneous thin or thick client platforms (e.g. mobile phones, tablets, laptops, and workstations).

Resource pooling. The provider's computing resources are pooled to serve multiple consumers using a multi-tenant model, with different physical and virtual resources dynamically assigned and reassigned according to consumer demand. There is a sense of location independence in that the customer generally has no control or knowledge over the exact location of the provided resources but may be able to specify location at a higher level of abstraction (e.g., country, state, or datacenter). Examples of resources include storage, processing, memory, and network bandwidth.

Rapid elasticity. Capabilities can be elastically provisioned and released, in some cases automatically, to scale rapidly outward and inward commensurate with demand. To the consumer, the capabilities available for provisioning often appear to be unlimited and can be appropriated in any quantity at any time.

Measured service. Cloud systems automatically control and optimize resource use by leveraging a metering capability at some level of abstraction appropriate to the type of service (e.g., storage, processing, bandwidth, and active user accounts). Resource usage can be monitored, controlled, and reported, providing transparency for both the provider and consumer of the utilized service.

Figure 8.2:   Listing of Cloud Computing Characteristics –
Essentially Predicted by Arthur C. Clarke
(Information from National Information and Standards
Institute - NIST)

As new capabilities such as the O3b satellite network (Note this stands for "Other Three Billion") that covers the developing world will make Internet in the equatorial region of the world much more accessible. Indeed as mobile satellite phone coverage via the latest generation of Inmarsat, Globalstar, and Iridium Next blanket the world, war and crimes against humanity will become increasingly hard to carry out in a covert manner. Today remote sensing satellites with time-stamped images are helping to prosecute war criminals in the Hague's International Criminal Court. Even in the most remote parts of the world "eyes in the sky" are maintaining a vigil over Planet Earth.

Clarke also saw the potential flip side of pervasive communications all over the world on a continuous basis. He did speculate about the consequences of global networking being all too tied together on a constant basis 24/7. He asked whether there might come a time when it would be illegal to turn off one's cell phone, or whether electronic signals might be used to control people in what he called the potential for "electronic possession of human brains."

He also acknowledged the potential of electronic information diarrhea and simple information overload. And clearly this too has become a major issue. Today a tiny percentage of information in a newspaper and its blog is actually consumed by a reader. The ratio of "passive information" that a person gets each day (i.e. unsolicited data) versus the amount of "active information" that they are actually seeking is probably at a level of 10,000 to 1. Governments wishing to cover up or withhold information in today's world of torrential data spewing out in Exabyte (i.e. a 1000 trillion bytes) chunks, might choose to bury it in a mountain of information as opposed to hiding it in a secure data bank.

Sociologist Robert Merton and Paul Lazarfeld did experiments on information overload with monkeys in the 1930s. They truly overloaded all of their sensory systems with amped up noise, white noise, blaring music, strobe lights and changing visuals. The result was apathy, loss of appetite, inability to sleep, loss of sex drive and eventually death. More recently researchers in Japan found that if a government wished to undertake an unpopular project in a particular area such as nuclear power plant or a hazardous waste disposal unit, the most effective strategy was not to create flyers and speaker bureaus to extol the benefits of such a project. No, the best strategy by far was to totally overload all media and information network channels with a huge quantity of "passive information" so that the citizenry and electorate simply turned a deaf ear to an overwhelming amount of data—too great to process. A recent critic of high definition television programs that are available in many countries 24 hours a day, 7 days as week said simply: "television is turning our brains into Corn Flakes."

Arthur C. Clarke has warned us that he slavish addiction to our electronic toys could be dangerous. His true zeal was to use the new electronic media to further the cause of effective global education and health care and other vital services that enriched rather than deadened the human brain. He recognized at a very basic level that all technologies can be employed for beneficial purposes and for negative causes almost with equal ease. A broadcast satellite can be used, as it is with "edsat" in India, to provide education to rural areas without schools. It would, however, be possible to "invert the technology" and install monitors on "subversive" so that broadcast satellites would become political monitoring devices to track those with unpopular views that opposed the programs of an entrenched set of political overlords.

Conclusions

Clarke thus insisted that it was important for scientists and engineers not only to develop new systems, but to assist leadership with moral choices to insure that the technology was used beneficially. In speeches to the United Nations, UNESCO, and other forums, he championed the use of technology to advance enlightened social goals. He did recognize that perhaps his most beloved technology, the geosynchronous satellite could at times be employed to saturate our brains with trivia, propagate the distribution of pornography, or to suppress antithetical political, social, cultural or religious views. Clearly in anticipating the Internet he foresaw an instrument of great social and economic impact, but he also warned about its averse applications as well—even before it had been invented.

Chapter 9

The Future of the City:
Telecommuting, Tele–education, and
Tele–health

"Computer-aided instruction--CAI—not to be confused with CIA—can be extremely effective. At its best, the pupil may refuse to believe that he is dealing with a computer program, and not another human being." **Arthur C. Clarke: <u>Spring—A Choice of Futures</u>, Ballantine Books, New York (1984).**

"We need mass education to drag this world out of the Stone Age, and any technology—any machine—that can help to do that is to be welcomed, not feared. The electronic tutor will spread across the planet as swiftly as the transistor radio, with even more momentous consequences. Nothing—no social or political system, no philosophy, no culture, no religion—can withstand a technology whose time has come...however much one may deplore some of the unfortunate side effects." **Arthur C. Clarke: <u>Spring—A Choice of Futures,</u> Ballantine Books, New York (1984).**

"The future of the electronic tutor has more to do with Mattel and Fisher-Price than it does with IBM." **Speech by Arthur C. Clarke at UNESCO on the occasion of the launch of the International Programme on the Development of Communications (1981).**

"Someday we may see a world in which a surgeon in Edinburgh, Scotland will be operating on a patient in New Zealand." **Arthur C. Clarke interview with the BBC in 1964.**

"In the future we will not have to commute, we will communicate….a person will be able to conduct their business from Haiti or Bali or anywhere they wish to live." **Arthur C. Clarke interview with the BBC in 1964.**

"…..if people didn't have to physically meet up, why would they choose to?" **from Time magazine story on Arthur C. Clarke, April 16, 1965.**

"Any teacher that can be replaced by a machine should be!" **Arthur C. Clarke, Electronic Tutors, 1980.**

It was Arthur's writings on many subjects that have helped to shape my thoughts on many subjects from energy to satellite communications, from time travel to what technology might move from the sphere of magic to reality within my life time. The quantum computers and direct communications between people using the brain's alpha waves are currently on my list of possible candidates. The area that has most consumed my thoughts and actions over the past twenty years is that of urban planning, the growth of global population and the social, medical, educational and economic use of tele-education, tele-medicine and telecommuting. These issues and technologies are key because of a world population, that in the words of Carl Sagan, has grown into the "billions and billions".

It is almost terrifying to realize that the numbers of humans on planet Earth have soared from 800 million in 1800 to 1.8 billion in 1900 to 6.3 billion as of 2000 and by 2100 may increase to 10 to 12 billion. The need to use tele-information in place of transportation has become increasingly evident in order to alleviate morning and evening traffic jams, to minimize climate change impacts on the biosphere, and to move ideas and information rather than people in an over populated planet. The concept of "electronic immigrant" that I developed in 1986/1987 in *Global Talk* and the *Futurist* magazine has certainly become today's reality. The idea of a telecity (again from *Global Talk* in 1986) and the metacity (from *The Safe City* in 2013) has not emerged as either Arthur C. Clarke nor I had originally envisioned. The constant movement of people into huge megacities, i.e. cities with more than 10 million people, has happened in spite of low cost and virtually free communications systems. The undisputed prime reason for this continued influx into the cities for now and for decades to come is clearly the pursuit of jobs and greater prosperity.

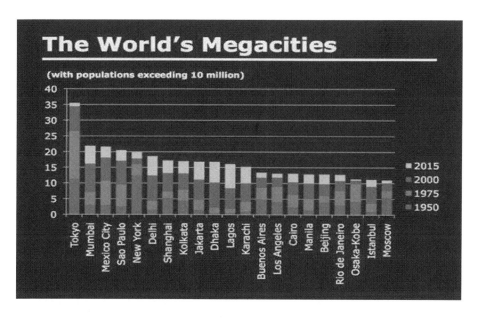

*Figure 9.1:   The Huge Surge in the Growth of Mega-Cities
(Source: I. Singh and J. Pelton, The Safe City (2013)*

The world human condition and current trend lines are incredibly out of whack due to:

•   Continued rapid increases to global population (Nigeria is poised to overtake the US as the world's third most populous nation; and the world will be perhaps 70% urban by 2050.)

• Rapid automation and increases in "super-automation" that can and will eliminate more jobs than new high tech enterprises will create.

• Increased consumption and higher standards of living worldwide (more calories consumed per capita, more cars per capita, more energy consumption per capita, more products and subsequent waste produced per capita.

• Increasing climate change, more violent storms, less potable water per capita, more energy and heat in the atmosphere.

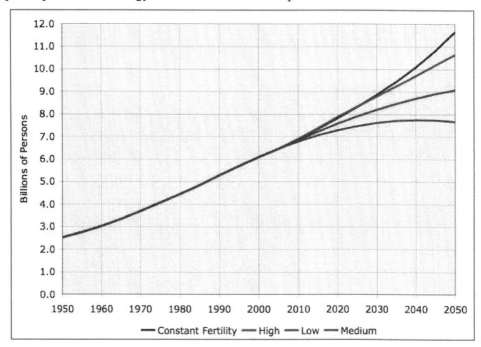

Figure 9.2: Runaway Global Human Population Growth from UN Study Projections
(Source: I. Singh and J. Pelton, The Safe City (2013)

In predicting that telecommunications will allow people to "communicate" rather than "commute", Arthur expected much more rational behavior to occur over the last 50 years. He thought that people would understand that smart machines and super-automation of manufacturing and service jobs via artificial intelligence would lead to less people being produced rather than more. He expected people to avoid flocking to core cities and to use telecommunications and IT systems to connect to the world and to service-based jobs. This would certainly have cost less rather than using energy-hogging transportation systems. The equation that the city somehow equates to jobs, negated this actually very logical expectation.

This is not to say that many have tried to move the city and urbanization toward telecommuting and to substitute the movement of information for the movement of people. The NEC corporation has created over 50 tele-commuting locations outside of the heart of Tokyo so that workers did not have to travel so far and over great distances. This was driven in large part by the huge cost of creating new office space in the heart of a megacity. Many large corporations such as AT&T, Hewlett Packard, IBM, insurance companies and even airlines like Jet Blue have created an information infrastructure to support large scale telecommuting. Environmental legislation has created incentives for employers to create telecommuting jobs. There are today over 1 million electronic immigrants that live in one country and work in another. Thus the trend lines that Arthur C. Clarke expected are indeed occurring in some countries such as the U.S., Japan and other developed countries, but more slowly than first anticipated. The laws to reduce urban pollution such as the U.S. Clean Air Act only require 10% of new development to be telecommunications based. Workers telecommute only one or two days a week because they fear that "out of sight is out of mind".

Of greatest concern of all is the rapid urbanization that continues apace in developing and industrializing countries where, according to the World Bank study figures, fully 80% of all new urban human settlement represents slums with inadequate access to transportation, water, sewage, health care and education. The rise of the tele-city may well occur decades hence, but first the very real problems of overpopulation, climate change, and automation and a dearth of jobs for the current supply of humans on the planet, must be understood, addressed and solved. We must understand that shutting down coal-fired power plants is no more than a totally inadequate band-aid. A surplus of people is the number one issue, whether the question is food, education, health care, urban planning, jobs, water supply, or protection against violent storms, natural disasters, or climate change.

It is in the area of tele-education and tele-medicine that Arthur C. Clarke's predictions are occurring much more rapidly. Countries around the world are moving to use IT and telecommunications to aid in the delivery of essential services key to human welfare. Countries such as Algeria, Brazil, China, Columbia, India, Indonesia, Korea (Rep. Of)   Malaysia, Mexico, Nigeria, Thailand, Turkey, as well as Australia, Canada, Europe, Japan, Russia, the United Kingdom, and the United States have elaborate and significant tele-education programs. Many of the programs are particularly geared to providing educational training to rural and remote areas and combine tele-health, practical training and nutrition information along with formal education programs. China and India alone have over 12 million students participating in satellite-based rural educational programs.

The Indian space program has launched dedicated INSAT spacecraft (i.e. the GSAT-3) to provide tele-education to remote villages throughout the subcontinent. The architecture of this extensive network provides a wide range of educational programs to Indian students via the aptly designated "Edusat" spacecraft.

Arthur C. Clarke not only predicted the widespread use of such networks but worked very closely with Dr. Yash Pal, of the Indian Space Research Organization and other educators to realize such systems in practice.

The combination of satellite-based education links that exist today can be intriguingly complex. The tele-education courses that are produced by the Chinese Ministry of Education and Central China Television are relayed by satellite to rural areas of China, but they are also downloaded on receiver earth stations in Sri Lanka and shipped by tape to western Iowa where they are again uplinked for American students to learn Chinese.

The Chinese satellite based tele-education program started in 1985 with experimental satellite broadcasts via the Intelsat Pacific Ocean Satellite. This initial program was started under what was known as the Satellites for Health and Rural Education (Project SHARE), that I headed while Director of Strategic Policy at Intelsat. as the substantive part of Intelsat's 20th anniversary celebrations. The initial tele-education broadcasts went to about thirty very small aperture terminals in very remote areas, but today there are over 90,000 such terminals.

While in Beijing with my colleague John Howkins, I asked just how remote were the villages being served? The answer was "very remote indeed". The satellite terminal was taken as far as possible by truck and unloaded. Then a group of villagers came and over a period of weeks carried the terminal to the even more remote village where it was powered by a gasoline powered electrical generator. Today there are scores of such satellite-based educational networks in operation around the world. The networks vary from very large to quite small, and from very simple to complex—both in terms of technology and course content

The U.S. Army Training Support Center now operates two networks which are the globally available, the Satellite Education Network (SEN) as well the Tele-training Network (TNET) that operates over the Internet. The largest shift in tele-education in the past decade has been the transition from satellite-based education and tele-health programming to Internet based programs. This has become possible as the Internet has reached further and further into remote and rural areas. The Jones International University is typical of this transition. Glen Jones, the head of Jones Cable Company in the U.S., started a tele-education program based on satellite distribution using the satellite antenna farm created to support his cable network in Centennial, Colorado as an off-shoot to his prime business. Glen Jones once called me to indicate that my writings on tele-education had helped to inspire him to start his now worldwide tele-education venture. As Internet access spread this was shifted over time to become an all on-line program. Today this is an accredited educational program operating in 44 countries and primarily offering MA & PhD degrees in Education and Masters in Business. Most open university programs today are distributed via terrestrial Internet links. Of course in rural and remote areas the Internet connection is still provided via satellite connections.

Despite the shift to Internet-based courses using terrestrial fiber, coaxial or cellular wireless technology, many significant tele-education programs via satellite remain alive and vibrant in Algeria, Columbia, Australia, Brazil, Canada, China, India, Indonesia, Japan, Malaysia, Mexico, Nigeria, Thailand, Turkey, the United States and many other locations. Many of these systems are highly asymmetrical in that the course lessons are downloaded via broadband streams but with only a limited upstream capability for student response or to ask questions. Open Universities, corporate training programs using business television (via fiber and satellite) and many other such educational and training programs continue to expand around the world. In the relatively near future with broadband services to "smart phones", and especially the new Fourth Generation-Long Term Evolution (4G-LTE) capabilities provided by the latest satellite interface standard known as Digital Video Broadcast-SH, will greatly enhance global opportunities for tele-education and tele-training services.

The latest high powered mobile satellite systems and the 4G terrestrial cellular systems will allow television training programs to flow to users all over the world via their smart phones. This is especially true of satellites optimized for Internet services such as O3b ("Other Three Billion" medium Earth orbit satellite network) which will widen the horizon for remote and rural tele-education and tele-health services all over the globe. The provision of tele-education and tele-training courses via the mobile Internet services (whether by satellite or terrestrial wireless) will likely expand ten-fold in just the next ten years because of its cost efficiency, increasing global reach, and the rapid expansion of course offerings available on-line.

Figure 9.3: Dr. James Legler in San Antonio, Texas views a blood slide from a rural town by means of video relay developed by NASA (Graphic courtesy of NASA).

Some of the tele-education networks that still exist by satellite, such as the University of the Caribbean and the University of the South Pacific, are significant in several ways. These telecommunications and IT based centers of learning serve as a "regional glue" to knit together a widely distributed group of small nations. These tele-linked institutions allow certain capabilities to be established and maintained throughout a region that would not otherwise be possible. This means, for example, that in the University of the Caribbean one campus in Jamaica can concentrate expertise in one area, another campus in the Dominican Republic can develope special skills in another discipline such as forestry and agriculture, while in Antigua or Aruba, the focus might be on water management and pollution.

Tele-medicine is typically much more challenging and difficult than tele-education because the many applications require much higher resolution for purposes such as making a correct diagnosis. Also there are other issues such as legal liability that make the use of tele-links much more problematic. Despite these issues, tele-medicine applications are growing—particularly in rural and remote areas where limited or no doctors or health services personnel are available. Technology that was initially developed by NASA for medical diagnosis for astronauts in orbit is now being routinely used in rural areas.

Conclusions

Arthur C. Clarke conceived of the geosynchronous satellite not as just a novel new technical tool, but rather as a potential instrument of change and development that could move the world forward. Clearly he saw the potential of satellites for broadcast entertainment, but he also anticipated that satellites could be deployed to rural and remote locations to provide education and training and health care in ways that would not be possible in any other ways.

There are many interesting and amusing stories as to how satellite-based educational and health care services were pioneered in Brazil, China, India, Indonesia and Malaysia. In India, for instance, the first experimental satellite transmissions on the ATS-6 satellite in the 1970s showed a public health film which explained how house flies carried germs. The villagers responded that they were glad that such enormous flies -- some apparently one foot long--did not exist in their village. The local health officials then had to explain television camera "close ups" and that the small flies in their village were indeed the same ones that were being shown in the film. In China, when I was Director of Project Share (Satellites for Health and Rural Education), I asked the Chinese officials in Beijing how they would ensure that the television programs would be watched in remote villages. They explained that the villagers as a group would spend perhaps a week carrying their satellite dish into its final resting place with enormous effort--sometimes carrying their load up and over mountain passes. These dishes weighed about 150 pounds (or 70 kilograms), The officials explained that after this much effort, they were pretty sure that the villagers would watch the programs, even if an unlucky someone had to pedal a bicycle-driven power generator. Since 1986 when the first experiments were carried out in China, however, a lot has changed and the current system that serves 10 million students is much more modern.

These programs have become more and more successful over time as the technology has become secondary to the services rendered to remote areas. Today satellite networks are increasingly linked to Internet systems in rural and urban areas alike. To Clarke, it would have made little difference whether a satellite VSAT dish or a Wi-Fi network was used to provide remote connectivity. The key was whether new electronic networks could be effectively used for education, health care, a link to the warning system for a coming tropical storm, or perhaps even for telecommuting to a distant job. Sir Arthur always recognized that it was the meaningful social application of a new technology that was the ultimate goal of human innovation.

Chapter 10

Cosmic Hazards and Planetary Defense

"....the rocket, far from being the destroyer of civilization may provide the safety valve that is needed to preserve it." **Arthur C. Clarke, The Exploration of Space, 1951.**

"I'm very fond of quoting my friend Larry Niven: 'The dinosaurs became extinct because they didn't have a space program. And if we become extinct because we don't have a space program, it'll serve us right!" **Arthur C. Clarke on Human Survival.**

"......one of the arguments for searching for intelligent life in space, elsewhere, is that we have no evidence that intelligence has any survival value. The most successful creatures on this planet are the cockroaches. They've been around, what is it, 100 million years or so and I suspect they'll still be there 100 million years in the future. Maybe intelligence is an evolutionary aberration which dooms its possessors in the way armor may have doomed some of the dinosaurs. **Arthur C. Clarke, Interview in 1995, Salon on line magazine, July 7, 2013**
http://www.salon.com/2013/07/27/arthur_c_clarke_scienc
e_fiction_writers_are_accidental_prophets_partner/

"After the asteroid hit on September 11, 2077 and destroyed Verona, Padua and also sunk Venice we set up Operation Safeguard". **Arthur C. Clarke, Rendezvous with Rama (1972).**

"Clarke was concerned about global climate change and what effect it may have on the future of humanity. He always stressed the urgent need for humanity to move beyond the use of fossil fuels, which he considered one of our most self-destructive behaviors. Yet Clarke was always optimistic about the future of humanity. "....the rocket, far from being the destroyer of civilization may provide the safety valve that is needed to preserve it"... in **"The Exploration of Space, 1951.**

"This is the first age that's ever paid much attention to the future, which is a little ironic since we may not have one." **Quotes of Arthur C. Clarke - Clarke Institute for Science Education.**

Arthur C. Clarke was wise in many ways. One of the many clever things he did was to provide his positive predictions about new technology, systems and concepts in his technical and more scientific books and writings. He then deftly provided his more dire warnings about giant disasters and possible horrendous events in his science fiction works. His most serious warnings about asteroid strikes thus came with his award winning *Rendezvous with Rama (1972)*. His warning about possible apocalyptic earthquakes came in *Richter 10* (1996), which Clarke wrote with Mike McQuay. His concepts about possible invasions by aliens came with the rather enlightened "overlords" in *Childhood's End (1953)*. Lore and literature can sometimes be a better basis for providing warnings to people or politicians who are in denial about the reality or possible consequences of disastrous events.

Clarke was concerned about many things. He was particularly concerned about green energy, strategies for the long term future survival of the human race and even the future evolutionary process that will inevitably lead to the next stage of intelligent life on planet earth. In fact what will be the next evolutionary step for humanity was one of his prime concerns. He believed that serendipitous mutation of human genes might provide us with new intelligence and new hope as a species. He felt even more strongly that artificial evolution of our intelligent machines would be the true breakthrough that would lead to an intelligence capable of leading humanity to long term survival against the many hazards that confront the Earth's fragile biosphere. Not only Arthur C. Clarke, but Carl Sagan, Ray Kurzweil and others have speculated as to whether human's are indeed smart enough to survive not only cosmic threats such as asteroids, comets, extreme solar events and cosmic radiation, but also other "internal human-generated planetary threats" such as chemical, nuclear or biological warfare, over population, over consumption of the Earth's resources or climate change.

Certainly many things worried Clarke about this quixotic and troublesome species known as *homo sapiens*. This list of concerns certainly included things like war and genocide, our intensive and seemingly wanton use of highly polluting carbon-based fuels, and the increasing vulnerability of advanced human technological society to cosmic destructive forces.

As a writer with a major focus on outer space, his prime focus on was on the tremendous power of cosmic hazards that could exceed by many orders of magnitude our largest nuclear weapons. He was indeed serious about the potential consequences of a large asteroid strike. He often quoted the following warning first provided by fellow writer Larry Niven.

> "*The dinosaurs became extinct because they didn't have a space program. And if we become extinct because we don't have a space program, it'll serve us right!*"

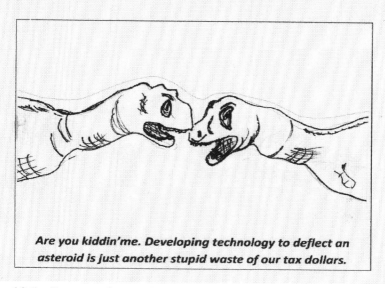

Are you kiddin'me. Developing technology to deflect an asteroid is just another stupid waste of our tax dollars.

Figure 10.1: Cartoon that reflects the warnings of Arthur C. Clarke and Larry Niven

When the U.S. Congress finally got around to funding the "Safeguard" program through NASA--and thus used the exact same name that Arthur gave to this undertaking in <u>*Rendezvous with Rama*</u> -- the scale of the program was actually modest. After launching the program with the initial aim of finding near earth objects one kilometer or more in size, the International Astronomical Union warned this was inadequate.

Thus in 2005 the U.S. Congress passed a bill known as the George E. Brown Jr. Near-Earth Object Survey Act. This legislation was signed into law as the NASA Authorization Act of 2005 and set specific objectives for NASA.   These Congressional mandated objectives included the need to define an upgraded identification program, involving both space and ground-based observation equipment. This expanded Safeguard Program would spell out a new effort for the identification and mapping of

Potentially Harmful NEOs and the idea was that such a plan would be quickly presented for Congressional approval. This law called for NASA to provide Congress with annual reports on progress toward these objectives, with the first such report being developed a year after the legislation went into effect and with new objectives established. This law also asked for updates with regard to possible strategies for deflecting potentially harmful objects. NASA finally produced the first such report in March 2007 that set forth the first clearly defined objectives for a program for identifying NEOs. The new goal in this new Safeguard plan was for NASA   to identify at least 90% of Near Earth Objects (NEOs) of 140 meters in diameter size by 2020, rather than the previous goal of identifying dangerous space rocks only down to a half kilometer. It also provided a detailed analysis of possible strategies for deflecting an asteroid or comet and evaluated their ability to accomplish this feat both for shorter term responses as well as responses that could be implemented over a longer-term period.

The specific language was to identify "by the end of 2020, 90 percent of all Potentially Hazardous Objects (PHOs) greater than 140 meters whose orbits pass within 0.05 Astronomical Units (AUs) of the Earth's orbit (as opposed to surveying for all NEOs)." (NASA Report to Congress). NASA, not surprisingly, has now confessed that it will not only miss this goal but do so by at least a decade. In many ways NASA has shown what many regard as a lackadaisical concern for cosmic threats.

Space Agencies and "Budgetary Fears".

At the March 19, 2013 hearing before the U.S. Congress House of Representatives Committee on Science, Space and Technology after the giant bolide strike in Siberia, Russia, NASA Administrator Charles Bolden explained that NASA would not be able to complete its survey of Near Earth Objects down to a diameter of 140 meters before 2030. He also referred to the Sentinel initiative of the B612 Foundation as a worthwhile effort but declined to suggest that NASA should play a direct role in the project. He indicated that if NASA were to take on this project it would cost perhaps $750 million while the B612 Foundation, as headed by former Astronaut Ed Lu and originally spearheaded by Apollo 8 Astronaut Rusty Schweickart, would likely be able to do the entire program for under $500 million. In short, the entire thrust of his testimony was: "Don't take away any of NASA budget allocations to spend money on detecting asteroids or planetary defense." The logic of course was perhaps in part that a cosmic catastrophe will most likely occur well after he had left office as NASA administrator.

On April 4, 2014 at a Washington Conference of System Engineers, I asked Administrator Bolden why none of the space agencies have established protecting the planet from cosmic hazards as a prime objective in their various strategic business plans. He smoothly deflected the question by saying that this was a serious issue that they took very seriously.

There are those, like Arthur C. Clarke, who take cosmic hazards that could wipe out modern infrastructure and cripple life as we know it quite seriously. The "we'll get around to it" attitude, not only of NASA but virtually all space agencies, is a bit baffling. Not one space agency today has in its strategic plan the planetary defense of Earth as a prime goal. None of the major space agencies are spending even one percent of their annual budgets on hazard detection and active mitigation. One might suspect that for the big space agencies the primary cause is "budgetary fear". This is firmly based on previous experience with their national legislatures. They know full well that if they asked for more resources to detect cosmic hazards and to develop new methods to deflect or mitigate the impact of potentially hazardous asteroids that it would come at the expense of their existing programs. As we all know the preservation of current budgetary funding levels is the top priority of any governmental agency around the world.

It is certainly not an accident that those who are leading the efforts to detect the threat posed by near earth asteroids   just happen to be astronauts who have been in space and seen just how vulnerable our small six sextillion ton planet just happens to be. Indeed astronauts are now able to look down and see what was very difficult to see from ground level.

In the 1980s a huge circular crater was discovered that is 180 kilometers across and 900 meters deep. This huge and perfectly shaped circular crater ranges along the coast of Mexico's Yucatan plateau and extends well out into the Gulf. By the 1990s space imaging was able to confirm that this was indeed the remnant of the giant asteroid that smashed into Earth. This event, which was the equivalent to the explosion of tens of thousands of nuclear bombs, blocked out the Sun with the cloud of dust that ensued. This was an event that we came to know as "Nuclear Winter", a phrase that came into popular usage during the Cold War era. This mass extinction event (now known as the K-T event) not only killed off the dinosaurs some 66 million years ago, but it also extinguished at least two-thirds of all plant and animal species that were alive on the day of this devastating impact.

***Figure 10.2: The massive crater left over from the so-called
K-T Mass Extinction Event
(Image Courtesy of NASA)***

This was Earth's Big Bang. What is unfortunately becoming more and more clear from recent scientific study is the likelihood that this type of massive and tragic event is much more likely than has been advertised for many years. A recent report that was devised from the global nuclear weapons monitoring system calculates that asteroid and bolide impacts on the planet occur ten times more frequently than previously thought.

What the B612 Foundation is undertaking is actually remarkable. They are trying to raise a half billion dollars to create a new "Sentinel" infrared space telescope that might be able to project forward for 100 years virtually all potentially hazardous objects that might hit Earth down to a diameter of not 140 meters (as in NASA's Project Safeguard program), not even 100 meters, but down to 30 meters to 40 meters. This is important because there are many more asteroids of this size than the larger space rocks that NASA is assigned by the U.S. Congress to detect.

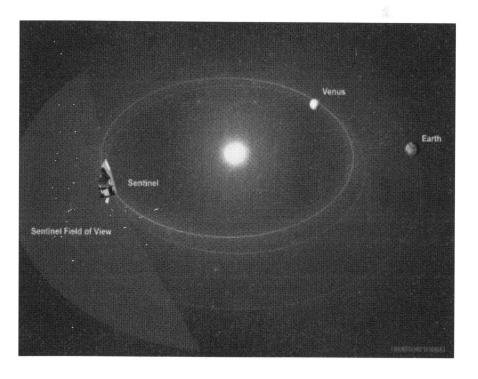

Figure 10.3: The Remarkable Sentinel Project to Detect Hazardous Asteroids (Source: B612 Foundation)

Why would the B612 Foundation be designing a spacecraft with an infrared telescope that could detect 30 to 40 meter asteroids beginning in 2017 or 2018 if NASA says it cannot complete an inventory of Near Earth Objects that are larger than 140 meters until at least 2030? The answer is the astronauts and staff at the B612 Foundation have a much clearer idea of the threat. They know that 30 to 40 meter asteroids are indeed "city killers". They know that a space rock of that size that enters the Earth's atmosphere traveling something like 28,000 kilometers per hour (or about 8 kilometers per second) has enormous kinetic energy.

If we assume that the asteroid only has a mass equivalent to water it would have a mass of 32,000 metric tons. A greyhound bus cruiser weighs around 40 metric tons. Just try to imagine 800 greyhound buses traveling not 100 kilometers per hour but 28,000 kilometers per hour. This is hard to imagine, but if the air burst occurred let's say 500 meters above New York or Washington, D.C., or London, Paris, or Beijing, the devastation would be enormous. Let's take the actual case of the recent Siberian air burst of the giant bolide over Siberia. This space rock was ten to fifteen times smaller than the 40 meter city killer that we have imagined and its velocity was also less, yet its kinetic energy was equivalent to 30 Hiroshima bombs.

There are clearly important differences between potentially hazardous asteroids and atomic bombs or we would truly be in for big time trouble. Atomic bombs are a lot nastier for several reasons. That first atomic bomb was detonated at 580 meters above Hiroshima, while the Russian meteor disintegrated over Siberia at altitudes 40 times higher than that of the Hiroshima detonation.   This made a huge difference as well as key variables related to heat and radiation. Yet the Siberian asteroid still packed the destructive power equivalent to 30 Hiroshima bombs in terms of kinetic energy. The "city killer" NEO asteroid would be something like 500 Hiroshima bombs and it would likely have an air burst explosion more like the Hiroshima experience. Clearly the big things to watch out for are the mass and velocity of the space rock and where it explodes in terms of altitude and proximity to the heart of the city. As the world's people density moves toward 70% urban and cities cover more and more of the planet our vulnerability is clearly shooting upward as well.

The detection of asteroids continues apace. With new technology our rate of detection has steadily increased with over 75% of the known NEOS discovered in the past decade with thousands of NEOS above 140 meters in diameter now known. But the estimates from the latest surveys and space systems such as the Wide-range Infrared Surveyor Explorer (WISE) and ground observations are alarming indeed. The B612 Foundation has indicated that there may well be 500,000 to a million NEOs that are in the category of 30 meters or more. NASA has a proposed program known as NEOCAM that would be able to help detect asteroids of larger size, but this program has yet to be funded.

At the urging of groups like the Planetary Society, the B612 Foundation, the Committee on the Peaceful Uses of Outer Space (COPUOS), Action Team 14 (that was charged by the UNISPACE III Conference to address cosmic threats), and others, the UN General Assembly acted in December 2013. In fact, the General Assembly took two specific actions to address the problem of asteroid and comet threats to Earth. First, they called for the creation of an International Asteroid Warning Network (IAWN) . The purpose of this Network is to make sure that all space-based and ground-based efforts to detect threats were integrated together to ensure all potentially threatening near earth objects are universally reported in a systematic fashion. And second, they further acted to create a Space Mission Planning Advisory Group (SMPAG) that would consult and advise on what type of protective action might be taken once a potentially hazardous asteroid is detected.

The truly disturbing fact to note is that potentially hazardous asteroids may not be the largest cosmic danger in terms of likelihood of occurrence. The largest threat may most likely come from extreme solar events such as solar flares that could damage our vital satellites, cause genetic mutation or create a higher incidence of skin cancer. Even worse than solar flares are so-called Coronal Mass Ejections (CMEs). These hugely powerful events can take out our power systems (as they did in 1989 with the so-called Quebec Event that took out the power grid and destroyed electrical transformers from Chicago to Montreal). In 2012 there was a so-called CME that would have rivaled the Carrington Event of 1859, but fortunately it largely bypassed earth. Had it come some days later who knows what destruction it would have brought to earth and to our modern infrastructure.

The 1859 event is the worst and most extreme Solar event currently on the record books. When this mega-event from the Sun occurred, trillion-tons rain of ions blasted the Van Allen Belts and our magnetosphere. It created a massive natural ElectroMagnetic Pulse (EMP). This explosive punch from the Sun set telegraph offices on fire and brought the "Northern Lights" down to Cuba and Hawaii.

We have no idea about what such an event would do to us today, but the bottom line is that we are not prepared. Likely results could include the loss of most of our communications, remote sensing, weather and navigation satellites, the destruction of most of the world's electrical transmission networks, the shutdown of the Internet, the grounding of most of our airlines, and perhaps the destruction of a great many of our computers and processors. This could close down most of the world's supply chains and millions of people might starve as we are socked back to near Stone Age conditions. If massive amounts of microprocessors were to be lost we would find that just about everything would stop working---cars, buses, trucks, aircraft, defense systems, washing machines, sewer and water systems, and just about everything else from banking to service industries around the world. Suddenly, almost everyone in economically developed countries would be unemployed and most people's skill sets would suddenly be useless. Executives and CEOs making millions of dollars a year would be much less valuable to society than farmers, huntsmen, or mechanics.

A massive CME could hurt us in many ways, but if it generated a massive ElectroMagnetic Pulse (EMP) that knocked out virtually all of our computers we would be dead in the water. Recently NASA scientist calculated what were the chances of a major CME punch hitting Earth within the next decade. The result of these calculations was a very disturbing 12% chance of our being hit with a massive amount of ions traveling at millions of kilometers per hour within the next ten years.

Arthur C. Clarke was one of the few science fiction/science fact writers who speculated on the dangers that could come to us from a dangerous and angry space attack—not from aliens, but from our Sun or a Near Earth Object (NEO). Once again, Clarke was ahead of the world's politicians and most of our scientists in suggesting that a planetary defense program needs serious attention and systematic global scientific and budgetary support from among the space agencies of the world. In today's world we have just reached the beginning stages of recognizing the extent of the danger. Currently what the UN General Assembly has done in creating the new International Asteroid Warning Network, (IAWN), a Space Missions Planning Advisory Group (SMPAG - pronounced 'same page'), and an Impact Disaster Planning Advisory Group (IDPAG) has only taken the first few baby steps. All of these groups would assist with international coordination of efforts to identify and response to NEO threats but this is actually only for starters.

These December 2013 UN actions give the impression that there could be a coordinated, effective and rapid response to a major asteroid strike, a coronal mass ejection that triggers an electro-magnetic pulse (EMP) that takes out our electrical power grid, or if some other cosmic catastrophe threatened. In fact, this is not the case. Unless there is a global force, modeled on UN peacekeeping operations with tens of thousands of first responders with special skills at the ready to respond we could be in for big time trouble. Nor is there a globally coordinated program that could rapidly move to divert an incoming asteroid. Likewise we have no effective ability to shield our planet from extreme solar events. This could become an increasingly severe concern, particularly if current shifts in the Earth's magnetosphere, that are currently occurring, leave us more vulnerable to extreme space weather in future years.

Conclusions

Clarke's expressed concerns in his scientific and sci-fi writings have led to the creation by NASA of a "Safeguard Program". Further his writings and expressed concerns may have helped to support the most recent United Nation's action to create the new asteroid warning and threat mitigation activities.

In addition Ministries around the world charged with homeland defense have established significant new programs to seek new and better ways to defend critical infrastructure against cosmic weather and extreme solar events such as coronal mass ejections and naturally triggered ElectroMagnetic Pulses (EMPs). These potentially deadly coronal mass ejections occur when billions (or even trillions) of tons of ion ejaculates from the sun hit the   Earth's magnetosphere. Despite these rather preliminary and truly "halting steps forward"   we still have a long ways to go. A program that is probably hundreds of times larger would be needed to create a true planetary defense system. At least some preliminary steps are now underway to create what Arthur C. Clarke, Larry Niven, Neil deGrasse Tyson, Apollo astronaut Rusty Schweickart and others have now strongly urged across many decades. (For more information on current efforts of this nature see: Charles L. Manto, *High-Impact Threats to Critical Infrastructure: Emerging Policy and Technology*, Dupont Summit Proceedings of the InfraGard National EMP SIG Sessions 2012.)

Chapter 11

The Clarke–o–sphere:
Facing up to the Social, Moral, and Cultural Considerations

"The information age has been driven and dominated by technopreneurs. We now have to apply these technologies in saving lives, improving livelihoods and lifting millions of people out of squalor, misery and suffering. In other words, our focus must now move from the geeks to the meek." **Arthur C. Clarke.**

"Perhaps the battle is already lost, here on this planet. As Sir George Darwin suggested in his depressing book, The Next Million Years, ours may be the Golden Age, compared with the endless vistas of famine and poverty that must follow when the billions of the future fight over Earth's waning resources. If this is true, it s all the more vital that we establish self-sustaining colonies on the planets. They may have a chance, even if civilization breaks down completely on the mother world." **Arthur C. Clarke, Profiles of the Future, (1962).**

"I would like to see us kick our current addiction to oil, and adopt clean energy sources. … Climate change has now added a new sense of urgency. Our civilisation depends on energy, but we can't allow oil and coal to slowly bake our planet." **Arthur C. Clarke.**

"As our own species is in the process of proving, one cannot have superior science and inferior morals. The combination is unstable and self-destroying". **Arthur C. Clarke.**

"During the Gulf war, comsats became the conscience of the world—a role already rehearsed in such global telecasts as the concerts to aid Bangladesh and Ethiopia. There is a danger, of course, that overexposure to disaster and tragedy will induce compassion fatigue, but the alternative—the indifference of ignorance—is surely worse." **Arthur C. Clarke, Epilogue, How the World Was One, (1992).**

"Another danger....is that all these wonderful new services will overload our capacity to absorb them. For there is more—much more—to come......bombarded with megabytes, we may simply switch off." **Arthur C. Clarke, Epilogue, How the World Was One, (1992).**

"....always remembering that information is not knowledge, and knowledge is not wisdom." **Arthur C. Clarke, Epilogue, How the World Was One, (1992).**

"Everyone recognizes that our present racial, political, and international troubles are symptoms of a sickness which must be cured before we can survive on our own planet. **Arthur C. Clarke, Report from Planet Three, (1972).**

"A hundred years ago, the electric telegraph made possible - indeed, inevitable - the United States of America. The communications satellite will make equally inevitable a United Nations of Earth; let us hope that the transition period will not be equally bloody." **Arthur C. Clarke.**

"The greatest tragedy in mankind's entire history may be the hijacking of morality by religion." **Arthur C. Clarke.**

For fifteen years Arthur C. Clarke served as the first and only Chancellor of the International Space University. This worldwide institution that now has over 5000 graduates from nearly 100 countries around the world has a unique perspective that is based on the so-called 3 I's---International, Intercultural, and Interdisciplinary. I was at the United Nations during the 1983 World Communications Years celebrations where my boss, Santiago Astrain, Director General of Intelsat and Sir Arthur C. Clarke were both speaking. As described earlier in Chapter one, it was there that I introduced Arthur to the three young founders of the ISU—Todd Hawley, Peter Diamandis and Bob Richards.

They were at the time promoting the Space Generation initiative as a global organization to bring young people into the realm of space and its utility to humankind. Young Todd Hawley who was finishing his Master's thesis on solar power satellites at George Washington University at the time was working for me as an intern at Intelsat. Todd was very impressed with the idea of how a commercially focused international entity like Intelsat could work so well across so many nations and cultures. He was just beginning to focus on the idea of how Intelsat might become a sort of model for an International Space University. Anyway those introductions of Arthur C. Clarke to the three founders of the ISU led to him agreeing to become Chancellor of the International Space University that had its organizing session in 1986 at the Massachusetts Institute of Technology.

The reason for this remembrance of over thirty years ago is this simply this. It was my own first unique insight into who Arthur C. Clarke really was.   His remarks at the United Nations back in 1983 and his signing on as Chancellor of the International Space University gave me a new insight into the very depth and breadth of Arthur C. Clarke as a human being. Arthur was not a space technologist. He was not a narrowly focused scientist. He was not a commercial science fiction or science fact writer. He was a humanist with a wide-ranging social conscience and all of his thoughts, writings, witticisms, scientific and sociological insights were a reflection of how interconnected he saw everything in a holistic fashion with both an intuitive insight and a moral compass. The immediate rapport that the three founders of the International Space University had with Arthur C. Clarke and to be immodest about it—myself—all centered around a holistic view of things. Their vision was not science, was not space, but seeing these issues in terms of what secrets of space and the universe could be unlocked in the context of international cooperation, intercultural understanding and interdisciplinary studies that related everything to everything else.

People who "don't get it" really do not understand what interdisciplinary studies, or systems analysis, or holistic thinking, or even looking at the big picture really means. In many ways Arthur C. Clarke was a practitioner of Zen. He would look at a thing and see how many things it could possibly be. He understood intuitively how everything the saw and sensed related to everything else. He considered everything not only in terms of its technical and scientific context, but what was the relevant social, moral, economic, and cultural context as well. The constant cultural clashes between the Tamil and Sinhalese peoples of Sri Lanka undoubtedly shaped the intercultural views of Arthur C. Clarke and his desire for harmony.

To Clarke the geosynchronous communications satellite was not a good in itself. It was good because it could unite the world, spread education, knowledge and health care across the world in new and unparalleled ways, and make political oppression and crimes against humanity increasingly difficult in a globally connected society.

"Morality ... Doesn't Require Religion At All"

In this chapter we seek to examine the dimensions of Arthur C. Clarke as humanist, a moralist, a social commentator, and a person with a strong conscience about technology and its impact on the human condition. For starters he was unapologetic about his views that extreme religious views were dangerous and something that humanity needed to outgrow.

Arthur actually tended to contrast rather than equate morality and religion. He notably said: "One of the great tragedies of mankind is that morality has been hijacked by religion. So now people assume that religion and morality have a necessary connection. But the basis of morality is really very simple and doesn't require religion at all."

As one reads about Clarke and his analysis and predictions about technology, it becomes clear over time that he also tends to look at new technical or scientific capabilities in the context of what good it can accomplish and how it can advance human civilization. To Arthur C. Clarke no man nor any one technology was an island. This he expressed in a variety of ways. One of my favorites was when he said: ""Before you become too entranced with gorgeous gadgets and mesmerizing video displays, let me remind you that information is not knowledge, knowledge is not wisdom, and wisdom is not foresight. Each grows out of the other, and we need them all."

Let's go back to Arthur C. Clarke's most famous predictions in 1945 in his "Extra-Terrestrial Relays" and the "Space Station" articles. One is struck by not only the technical detail and precision of the prediction---from which over 30 further predictions were enumerated—but by his examination of the societal uses that might be derived from his proposed geosynchronous and even lower earth orbit satellite constellations. He talked about the social and economic utility of global television, of mobile telecommunications to rural and remote areas not now reachable. He envisioned communications with aircraft flying in pathways where terrestrial telecommunications would be difficult and exact space navigation, such as the GPS network provides today. He also thought about the use of geo satellites for global meteorological survey and prediction, and the utility of low cost user terminals for telecommunications on a completely global basis. In fact, it is difficult to find any of Arthur C. Clarke's predictions where he discussed the technology without considering the social and economic implications. This was true in his discussion of satellite communications, weather satellites, and new energy sources--such as ocean thermal energy conversion or nuclear fusion. It was also true of transportation systems, urban planning and telecommuting, tele-education and tele-health. Further he spent a good deal of time analyzing the impact on society that would come with computers, information networking, robotics, bioengineering, and agriculture. He considered not only the social benefits as is not often the case with technologists, but he also considered the possible dark sides as well. He often addressed the social or economic harms, the loss of privacy, the wartime uses, and the potential to give rise to oppressive government that might come with his latest thoughts about new applications of technology.

The following (Table 11.1) is a chart that seeks to provide a systematic review of Arthur C. Clarke's predictions over a wide range of areas, and his assessments—both positive and negative--of the wide range of technologies and systems that he addressed during his ninety years here on Planet Earth..

Table 11.1

Arthur C. Clarke's Predictions and His Assessments of their Potential to Do Good or Harm

Prediction	Application	Potential for Good	Potential for Harm
Geo Satellite Communi- cation (1945)	Television Distribution	Global televisionews Freedomfrom tyranny Rural and remote connectivity Low cost user terminals	Information overload
Mobile Communi- cations (incl. mobile satcoms (1952)	Communicatio ns to aircraft Communicatio n to vehicles & remote areas.	More efficient routing and ability to maneuver around storms	Loss of privacy Big Brother Government surveillance
Satellites for Navigation (1945/1952)	Navigation for aircraft, ships & vehicles	Avoidance of dangers and more efficient travel paths	Personal tracking of dissidents

Meteoro-logical Satellites (1945)	Prediction of dangerous weather	Saving of lives of people and livestock Avoidance of flooding	Overdevelopment of unsafe areas
Free flow of information on global networks.	Unrestricted news and global updates in real time	Accurate updates on crimes against humanity and atrocities.	Spread of pornography and hate messages
"Thinking " computers, robotics and cyborgs (1958 & 1968)	Safety measures Reduction in work Labor saving in farming mining, manufacturing and service industries	More leisure time. Use of machines to carry out dangerous tasks	Under-employment, Use of machines to impose rule on people, robotic warriors
Automated cars (1972)	Improved personal transportation	Traffic safety and elimination of traffic jams	Too many cars and atmospheric pollution
Nearly free and abundant energy based on non-fossil fuel sources	Ready supply of energy. Possibility of low cost space travel and ability to undertake planetary re-engineering	Replacing of "dirty" fossil fuels with clean energy. Potential to end poverty and end neediness	Could contribute to overpopulation and over consumption in other areas.
Low cost and computer & telecom enhanced education	Delivery of quality tele-education to rural and remote areas	Global literacy	Rising economic expectations without commensurate Opportunity
Low cost and computer & telecom enhanced medicine	Delivery of quality tele-medicine to rural and remote areas	Global quality health care	Overpopulation

Planetary Defense Systems against cosmic hazards	The Safeguard Program to warn against comets and asteroids	Global defense mechanisms and more effective disaster warning systems	False sense of security. Overlooking of space weather dangers
A city based on computers and telecommun- ications	Improved traffic systems. Fire control systems. Smarter housing and offices.	Improved traffic flow and less natural and man-made disasters. Less pollution. Less criminal & terrorist activities.	Big brother surveillance and oversight. Less human innovation and initiative.
A peaceful and united world civilization	A global society that allows peaceful world unity	A world without bloody wars	A world that is stagnant and does not advance.
Low cost access to space	Space elevators or funiculars allowing easy and low cost access to space	Improved communications, navigation, weather forecasting, and resource monitoring. Space colonization.	Orbital space debris. Over exploitation of Earth's resources.
Replacement of chemical rockets to access to space	Improved and lower cost space applications & exploration systems.	Reduction of space debris. Reduction of atmospheric pollution	Increases in orbital debris
Solution to world's environmenta l pollution problems	Clean energy, Improved habitats and offices. Clean transport systems.	Reduced atmospheric and oceanic pollution. Healthier environment. Prevention of global destruction and end of the human race on Earth.	Renewed tendency to overpopulate

This is not a complete list of all of the technologies, systems and concepts that Arthur C. Clarke addressed in his science fact and science fiction writings and video productions, but it is sufficiently exhaustive to show the breadth and depth of his thinking. The many writings and explorations that he made with regard to energy were driven by his thoughts that it was the lack of clean and plentiful energy that held humankind back from achieving its eventual potential. Later in his life, Arthur devoted a good deal of his attention to clean, cheap and plentiful energy supplies as critical to the future of humanity. He spent a good deal of time on so-called Low Energy Nuclear Reactions (LENR) or Chemically Assisted Nuclear Reactions (CANR), Ocean Thermal Energy Conversion, Nuclear Fusion, as well as solar energy. He even dabbled in such far out ideas as "anti-gravity" as a clean transportation system. He did not examine or speculate in these various fields because he was infatuated by these technologies *per se*. He pursued these studies and forecasts because of the social and economic implications. He saw the need for clean, cheap and abundant energy as the tonic that could set humans free to realize their potential.

To Arthur it was fossil fuel energy that carried the threat of disastrous climate change and species annihilation, made living and transportation expensive, and was the source of great poverty in a modern world. When asked in an interview in 2007 by the *Futurist* as to what he would wish for the future, his simple three wishes were as follows. He wished for contact with extraterrestrial life, for world peace and for clean and plentiful energy. Here is how he put it precisely: "Cleaner energy sources for the future of civilization, here and beyond Earth."

Conclusions

It was not one of Arthur's laws that one should be careful as to what you wish for, but this was always a part of his thought process when he forecast a new technology or capability. He—the great and glib generator of grist for the global media—often provided sardonic quotes about his misgivings about technology and where it might take us. During his lifetime Arthur C. Clarke commented from a social, economic and moral perspective on just about everything. Topics on which he expressed a view included just that, as summarized below:

- The ruinous consequences of automobile and over consumption of petroleum
- The hazards of over consumption of vanishing resources
- The pollution of the atmosphere and the oceans
- The horrendous nature of nuclear weapons and modern warfare
- The need to extend education and health care on a global scale to a much broader audience
- The use of technology to expose political corruption and crimes against humanity
- The need for automation to control traffic and stop traffic deaths
- The ability of modern satellites to create completely mobile communications that includes navigation and search and rescue so no one will ever be lost and airlines could   fly more safely
- The utility of electronic communications and computer networks to extend health care, banking, market efficiency, and human welfare in general.
- The worrisome ability of totalitarian states to use satellite and other technology for surveillance and to exercise oppressive control of their people.
- The price of open networks and the non-exercise of censorship which gives rise to the flow of hateful messages and pornography, but then he concludes that the alternative of regulated networks is much worse. If Arthur C. Clarke lived in the U.S. he would likely have considered joining the American Civil Liberties Union.

In   Annex A below are just a sampling of a few more of his quotes on social, moral or ethical issues. His moralistic musings outnumber his predictions by a goodly number.

ANNEX A
Arthur C. Clarke's Social Conscience in Play

"Remember that the United States was created by two inventions—the railroad and the telegraph. If we are not careful, it may be destroyed by a third—the automobile."

""...no one on the planet need ever get lost or become out of touch with the community, unless he wanted to be. I'm still thinking about the social consequences of this!"

"From their perches in orbit, Landsats and Seasats allow us to look at our planet with new eyes, surveying instantaneously all its agricultural, mineral and hydrological resources. And, equally important monitoring their misuse."

".....we'll certainly have to get rid of the gasoline engine, and everybody is now waking up to urgent necessity of this. Apart from the facts of air pollution, we have much more important uses for petroleum."

"The only defence against the weapons of the future is to prevent them ever being used."
"I can see a time when it will be illegal for a human being to drive a car on a main highway."

"We need mass education to drag this world out of the Stone Age, and any technology—any machine" that can do that is to be welcome, not feared."

".....the Telephone in the Village would be one of the most effective force multipliers in history. Because of the implications for health, animal husbandry, weather forecasts, market advice, social integration and human welfare."

"...with the free flow of information .....no government will be able to conceal, at least for very long, evidence of crimes or atrocities—even from its own people."

".... could there come a time when it is a crime to switch off one's mobile phone?"

Part II:

Clarke's Predictions for

Tomorrow

Chapter 12
Advanced Artificial Intelligence and Von Neumann Machines

*"It is even possible that the first genuine thinking machines may be grown rather than constructed; already some crude but very stimulating experiments have been carried out along these lines. Several artificial organisms have been built which are capable of rewiring themselves to adapt to changing circumstances. Beyond this there is the possibility of computers which will start from relatively simple beginnings, be programmed to aim at specific goals, and search for them by constructing their own circuits, perhaps by growing networks of threads in a conducting medium. Such a growth may be no more than a mechanical analogy of what happens to every one of us in the first nine months of our existence.***" Arthur C. Clarke, Profiles of the Future, Guernsey, Great Britain (1988).**

"It is too late to worry about if computers will take over the world. Let us hope that our silicon successors will treat us kindly." **Arthur C. Clarke Interview with Representatives from the Internet Society in Sri Lanka, April 2002.**

"Timeline 2020: Artificial Intelligence reaches human level. From now on there are two intelligent species on Earth." **Arthur C. Clarke, "Beyond 2001" Reader's Digest, February 2001.**

"…..people that say we will never develop computer intelligence — they merely prove that some biological systems don't have much intelligence." **Interview with Arthur C. Clarke. L.A. Review of Books, 1995.**

One of the most enduring images from the movie "2001: A Space Odyssey" is the scene in which Dave is shutting down HAL9000 by disconnecting its circuitry and memory banks. HAL's lines: "My mind is going. I can feel it." are quite poignant because it sounds as if a person or at least a sentient being is dying. Clarke, however, with his typical impish humor attached a recording to his computer that automatically played these lines from the movie when he shut his computer off. The images of HAL from the movie conveyed to the public the idea that someday machines with artificial intelligence would not only "think" but that they would "feel" emotions like anger, fear, angst, pain and perhaps even love. The ability for human intelligence to create true artificial intelligence, as anticipated by Clarke, is coming closer each day. As we will explore in this chapter the latest estimate is that this will indeed become possible as of 2023 less than a decade from now.

Figure 12.1: Heuristic Algorithm 9000
(Image courtesy of Frederick Ordway)

In *Profiles of the Future* in 1988, Arthur C. Clarke speculated on how the evolutionary path of human beings would unfold and suggested that an artificial evolutionary process driven by machine intelligence could be much, much faster since it would not depend on chance mutations, but rather on sophisticated artificially intelligent programs searching for positive innovation. In this environment where trillions of innovations could be processed and evaluated within a single hour, the rate of evolution would increase at an ever faster, exponentially expanding rate. Clarke has even speculated on the premise that virtually any conceivable technology that did not break the laws of physics could be achieved within the next three hundred years. He has suggested that ultimately, rather than humans being ruled by the stars, someday humans may even rule the stars by conquering the secret to controlled nuclear fusion.

Indeed in his book *2010: Odyssey Two* Clarke envisions a vastly superior alien intelligence as being able to deploy an array of von Neumann machines that are able to compress the vast giant gaseous Jupiter in a controlled network fashion and to ignite a second star within the solar system so that a new intelligent life form can evolve more quickly on Jupiter's moon Europa.

As Clarke described, through this process there could be rapid evolution of human thought and science, but that there could also be a superior machine intelligence as well. He projected the evolution of a silicon-based intelligence that could exist within a new type of bio-engineered body. This, in his conception, would represent an evolved being superior to human capabilities in every way—higher intelligence, freedom from disease, and not prone to war and violence. Not only would these "evolved beings" have greater skills, but they would be able to achieve a sort of global omnipresence and terrestrial omnipotence that would transcend human's currently limited sense of time and place.

Here is how Clarke actually put it: "One can imagine a time when men who still inhabit organic bodies are regarded with pity by those who have passed on to an infinitely richer mode of existence, capable of throwing their consciousness or sphere of attention instantaneously to any point on land, sea, or sky where there is a suitable sensing organ. In adolescence we leave childhood behind; one day there may be a second and more portentous adolescence, when we bid farewell to the flesh."

Today, Ray Kurzweil has, as much as any AI guru, inherited from Dr. Marvin Minsky the mantle of "Mr. Artificial Intelligence". He has proposed—in close coincidence with Clarke's prediction that machines equal to human intelligence would be around in 2020-- that this breakthrough in artificial intelligence will come as early as the 2020s. In his book *The Singularity is Near* , Kurzweil has specifically defined this milestone as coming when artificially intelligent machines are able to exceed the capability with the thinking power of a human with an IQ of 100. Certainly milestone after milestone has now come and gone. IBM's Deep Blue was able to defeat the world's best chess Grand Master Garry Kasparov back in 1997. This was predicted by Clarke in 1968 when he had the supercomputer HAL 9000 showing its ability to defeat humans in the film *"2001: A Space Odyssey"*. Then IBM's Watson© in February 2011 was able to defeat, by a wide margin, both Ken Jennings and Brad Rutter, the top two money winning contestants in the history of the game show Jeopardy.

Today IBM is using Watson AI capabilities to take on job after job in the highly trained and skilled service industry. At one time many of these professions were reserved for only highly capable and well educated humans, but this is no longer true. "Watson", or other forms of expert systems or AI , are   now being used by doctors to make diagnoses, by statisticians to project consumer behavior, and by ad agencies to design advertising campaigns. In the case of medical applications, Watson is currently being upgraded to "read and include" in its memory banks billions of medical articles to make a "Dr. Watson" version of this petabyte interactive data base. In short, the new version of Watson will be the world's most comprehensive medical brain. All one has to do is access this specialized Watson data base and the "Doctor" is in.

The future that Arthur C. Clarke envisioned in terms of the "breakthrough" that occurred in *Childhood's End* may only be only a decade away.

There are essentially three elements that one would need to access super-intelligence. These are essentially virtually infinite memory capabilities, unlimited and instantaneous global access to such vast databases, and the ability to process a myriad of intellectually coherent algorithms at incredible speed.

- Infinite Memory: The Watson technology allows nearly instantaneous access to an ever growing wealth of accumulated knowledge. The process now underway to accumulate virtually all known medical information in an expanded version of Watson is the bow wave of the future in this regard.
- Instantaneous Global Access: Today's Internet, intranets, fiber networks, satellite and broadband cellular networks allows access to information at amazing speeds and at an incredible geographic range. It is possible to glue together the world's astronomical observatories so that the entire planet Earth can become a giant telescope. We are rapidly evolving toward omnipresence capabilities.
- Infinite Processing of Complex Thinking Algorithms: This is today the limiting capability. We are not limited by teraflops or broadband networking, but by our heuristic algorithm capabilities.

Ray Kurzweil, previously introduced, is perhaps today's most advanced thinker on artificial intelligence and our ability to extend the neocortex capability of the human brain. Here is how he anticipates future progress in his book _How to Create a Mind: The Secret of Human Thought Revealed:_ "I estimated earlier that we have on the order of 300 million pattern recognizers in our biological neocortex. That's as much as could be squeezed into our skulls even with the evolutionary innovation of a large forehead and with the neocortex taking about 80 percent of the available space. As soon as we start thinking in the cloud, there will be no natural limits—we will be able to use billions or trillions of pattern recognizers, basically whatever we need."

Kurzweil goes on to explore the consequences of this type of artificial extension of the thinking capability of the human brain thusly: " In order for a digital neocortex to learn a new skill, it will still require many iterations of education, just as a biological neocortex does, but once a single digital neocortex somewhere, and at some time, learns something, it can share that knowledge with every other digital neocortex without delay."

According to research carried out by Professor Henry Markham's Blue Brain Project we are closing in fast on a machine version of a fully functioning human brain. Markham's research team reports remarkable progress in terms of achievable computer memory and computer speeds that are, as of 2013, reported to be the equivalent of a rat's brain by being able to achieve 10^{15} (or) or peta flops in processing speed and 2×10^{14} (or 200 terabytes) in computer memory. Markham's current projection is that in 2023 his team will have moved a thousand times forward and achieved the ability to simulate the equivalent of a human brain's processing capability. Incidentally, this capability Markham equates rather non-prosaically to about 10^{17} (or 100 petabytes) in memory and 10^{18} (or exaflops) in computer processing speed. In Markham's equation the human brain = 1000 rat brains = 100 trillion synapses.

This calculus on the part of Markham's research team leads to some profound questions. One of the first questions would be whether it is realistic to project that a simulated human brain can actually be achieved in 2023.   It seems that it is quite ambitious to go from a rat brain in 2013 to a 1000 times greater functionality in just nine years.

The other more profound question is that if we can, in the future, access not only trillions or even quadrillions of digital neurons, what would such a "thinking machine" be able to do? Could it perhaps simulate a million rat brains or the equivalent of a thousand human brains? What would such an 'intelligence' be able to accomplish?

And why stop there? In the cloud of the future we might even devise a super digital neocortex equivalent to a million human brains. Could such a super brain find the solution to infinite, free and non-polluting power?

Or the cure to cancer? Or accomplishing what we now consider to be impossibilities such as teleportation, reanimation of the dead, anti-gravity or perpetual motion machines, or even transiting a black hole? Such puzzles we can only contemplate since Clarke in *Childhood's End* never revealed what the mind-meld intelligence of the global brain was actually able to accomplish.

If we can go from a rat's brain to a human brain simulation—a 1000 fold increase in just nine years—i.e. from 2014 to 2023—why not a million-fold increase in two decades or a billion-fold increase in three decades? What if an ultra-smart super computer that can simulate a million human brains figures out that it is humanity that is infecting planet Earth? According to James Lovelock, who developed the visionary view of Earth as GAIA, this seems to be exactly what is happening. *Homo sapiens* are indeed threatening all life forms due to overconsumption, runaway climate change, and pollution of the oceans and the stratosphere. Does the super brain not only diagnose the problem but also develop technology to reduce human population or eliminate the "human virus" that is infecting Earth altogether?

Even if Henry Markham's team and the Blue Brain Project do not succeed, it seems likely that others will. In laboratories around the world, system analysts and researchers are building faster and faster computers. These computers will be able to access memory at faster and faster rates. Elsewhere programmers are creating learning protocols with more and more adept learning processes (i.e. heuristic algorithms). Vast networks that are increasingly broadband are sharing this information ever more widely. The perfect storm of artificial intelligence connected to a cloud with nearly infinite processing power suggests that Arthur C. Clarke may well have been right when he created in his book *Childhood's End* the literary image of intellectual "breakthrough" into the form of all the young progeny of planet Earth linked together as one giant "global brain". When he suggested that virtually all forms of technical and scientific knowledge could be achieved within three hundred years he may have proved again his theory that very long term predictions turn out to be too cautious. What is clear is that the latest work that is being pursued by Markham, Kurzweil and others would argue that Clarke's conception of a giant global brain may indeed be just a decade or so away from realization.

Conclusions—Intelligence versus Survival

Too often we look to the future through a rear view mirror and make the assumption that human civilization is on a linear path.   Arthur C. Clarke is one of the few that recognized that innovation tends to follow an exponential path. His other perhaps even more profound observation was that such geometric progressions are almost always unstable. Growth patterns in natures that do not eventually switch over from geometric growth to a more stable curve that resembles the shape of an "S" simply do not survive. When we talk about sustainability we often forget this most basic biological rule of survival. This thus returns us to Clarke's basic question. This is whether intelligence and survival are linked or not? Does, in fact, intelligence always lead to instability? The known species that have lasted the longest, such as beetles for instance, are perhaps lowest on the intelligence scale.

Chapter 13

Ground, Air and Space Transportation Concepts

Prediction for 2095 - The development of a true "space drive" - a propulsion system reacting against the structure of space time -that makes the rocket obsolete and permits velocities close to that of light. The first human explorers set off to nearby star systems that robot probes have already found promising. **Arthur C. Clarke, The 21st Century Beyond 2000, Asia Now.**

"Vannemar Morgan's dream is to link Earth to the stars with the greatest engineering feat of all time—a 24,000 mile high space elevator. But first he must solve a million technical, political and economic problems." **<u>Foundations of Paradise",</u> Arthur C. Clarke, (1952).**

".....spaceship Discovery uses the "perturbation manoeuvre" to harness the gravitational pull of Jupiter to "slingshot" the craft towards Saturn. **<u>"2001: A Space Odyssey", Arthur C. Clarke,</u> (1968).**

"I believe that the Golden Age of space travel is still ahead of us. Before the current decade is out, fee-paying passengers will be experiencing sub-orbital flights aboard privately funded passenger vehicles, built by a new generation of engineer-entrepreneurs with an unstoppable passion for space. We are seeing the emergence of a new breed of 'Citizen Astronauts' and private space enterprise." - **Arthur C. Clarke in 2001.**

"Ground Effect Machines (GEMs) can move backwards or sideways simply by altering the direction of their air blasts and will normally float at an altitude of ten feet. This will enable them to skim smoothly over all but the very roughest seas, so they could be quite lightly constructed and would, therefore, be much more efficient than sea bourne ships, which must be built to withstand enormous stresses and strains.......with the emancipation of traffic from the road, we will have at last achieved true mobility on the face of the Earth." **Arthur C. Clarke in *"Profiles of the Future"* - chapter 4 "Riding on Air" (1988).**

".. out to Jupiter employing spacecraft equipped with 'the Sakharov drive' that employs nuclear fusion"..... ***"2010: Odyssey Two", Arthur C. Clarke, (1982).***

"Then antigravity was invented and you could move goods or houses or anything else through the sky without bothering about geography." ***"The Songs of a Distant Earth", Arthur C. Clarke, (1958).***

Arthur C. Clarke must have suffered many disappointments as a direct result of his futurist dreams. It must be frustrating indeed to see clearly what might be, assess when it it is likely to be -- and then not being able to see it realized within his lifetime. This must have been particularly galling in cases where the necessary technological and engineering capabilities were there but social, economic or business interests intervened to stop progress in a particular direction.

What Arthur dubbed the "Ground Effect Machine" (GEM) must have particularly been such a case of very great disappointment indeed. Arthur explained very clearly and in some technical detail how what might be described as the equivalent of a powerful inverted fan could be utilized to create an all-purpose hovercraft. This Ground Effect Machine, as envisioned by Clarke could serve as an efficient transport system to carry people and cargo over land, swamps, deserts, rivers, lakes and oceans. He explained in a full chapter of *Profiles of the Future* how these devices could save the cost of constructing roads and bridges and hugely expensive freeway interchanges. He eloquently argued how these Ground Effect Machines could be more efficient and lower in cost than ships and cars and highway networks. He also explained how such systems could also be much safer than aircraft since they could gently descend ten feet (3 meters) to the ground in the case of mishap. (The issue of mishap at sea was not addressed, but an inflatable GEM life raft could undoubtedly have been devised.)

Clarke's grand vision of hovercraft that could move all over the world without the need for roads, freeways, airport landing strips, etc. has never come to pass. This could be put down to several factors. Perhaps the largest one would be the disruptive nature of the business interests involved in building aircraft, ships, automobiles, and road systems plus the oil and gasoline industries that are firmly entrenched behind all of these transportation systems. The practical question of traffic control and how billions of people could safely navigate in such a GEM dominated travel system would certainly have presented another major problem to be solved, but as one wit has suggested, perhaps just working out how fish swim without colliding could produce a quite valid answer.

Even some forty years after his original predictions in the early 1960s, Clarke still asserted that this universal-use type hovercraft still made enormous sense. He started out by explaining that this exact same technology had indeed been developed to move heavy oil machine drilling equipment in the arctic regions. He noted that in the arctic North where roads were not available this very versatile technology had been called into play. There a high velocity turbofan system was invoked to ferry multi-ton oil rigs across the Alaskan tundra where it was impossible to build roads.

But Arthur was still not one to tilt at wind mills. When I visited him in Sri Lanka his driver ferried him around in a spiffy red Mercedes. Also we did go for a ride in an ultralite designed by the very same man who designed micro-aircraft for the James Bond movies—in addition to Burt Rutan. I suppose that this was as close as he ever got to riding in a Ground Effect Machine.

Commercial Space Travel - Prospects and Setbacks

Clarke may have been wrong about the ground effect machine as a future transportation system, but he was very much on target in seeing the potential of commercial space ventures. Today we are seeing a number of these new type commercial space ventures come together in rather amazing ways. There are now spaceplanes able to carry "citizen astronauts" into space on sub orbital flights above 100 kilometers (i.e. SpaceShipTwo, XCOR Lynx, etc.). There are successful flights to the International Space Station that have resulted from the NASA's Commercial Orbital Transportation Systems undertaking. The Space X-developed Falcon 9 launcher and the Dragon Capsule, as well as the Orbital Sciences Corporation-developed Antares launcher with its Cygnus capsule are today delivering cargo and off- -loading waste from the International Space Station (ISS) on what now seems almost routine missions. And now, in the Fall of 2014, SpaceX (the start-up company pioneered by Elon Musk) and the Boeing Corporation have been selected by NASA to further commercialize space. However, there was a major set-back to the SpaceX program in October 2014 when the second of its delivery missions to the ISS suffered a malfunction and was destroyed shortly after lift-off.

These two aerospace companies are set to develop commercial crew delivery systems to take astronauts to and from the International Space Station as well. It seems significant that for doing essentially the same development work and carrying out astronaut deliveries to the ISS, on a new commercial crew delivery system, that the Boeing Corporation Contract was nearly $5 billion or about twice the amount of the contract for the start-up Space X.

There are also pending capabilities that will allow new space systems to fly satellites and spacecraft into orbit. Here the options include the SpaceShip Two small mission launcher being developed by by Sir Richard Branson's Virgin Galactic and the SpaceShip Corporation. But again, there was a major disaster in October 2014 when the spacecraft exploded during a test flight over the Mojave Desert in California. The pilot was killed the the co-pilot was seriously injured after ejecting. There is a full inquiry into the cause and Branson has said that if the problems that caused the crash are overcome, the his plans for 'space tourism' would continue.

Using a much different type single stage to orbit the Reaction Engines' Skylon space plane also plans to be able to fly to low earth orbit. Then there is the amazing Stratolaunch project to provide the world's largest aircraft carrier system that will be powered by six 747 aircraft engines. This "carrier vehicle" will support larger rocket launch systems. To date about 500 astronauts have flown into space from astronaut and cosmonaut programs sponsored by NASA, Roscosmos, and the Chinese Space Agency as well as flights by astronauts supplied from many other space agencies around the world. On the basis of commercial space flights, however, we are going to shortly transition into a new age. In this new age, as foreseen by Clarke, thousands of "citizen astronauts" are likely to fly into space in the next decade.

In the last few years an emerging group of "space billionaires" have worked to realize the dream of developing commercial space—and in remarkably short order. This started with Paul Allen of Microsoft fame who financed Burt Rutan's design of SpaceShipOne that won the $10 million Ansari XPrize in 2004.

Then came the most notorious of them all, the British balloonist, Virgin entrepreneur, private island owner and multi-billionaire Sir Richard Branson. He chose to use the Spaceship Two, developed from the XPrize enterprise, and founded Virgin Galactic which promises to fly hundreds if not thousands of citizen astronauts into space on high arcing sub-orbital flights.

Figure 13.1: Burt Rutan, Designer of SpaceShipOne and Space Billionaire Paul Allen
(Graphic Courtesy of Ansari XPrize)

Yet another space entrepreneur is the South African Elon Musk, who made his first fortune by co-founding PayPal and went on to start SpaceX in order to realize his dream of commercial space travel and ultimately sending people to Mars. As noted earlier, the SpaceX company developed the Falcon 9 and Dragon Capsule launch system that delivers cargo to the International Space Station and now will develop an even more reliable crew delivery system to fly astronauts to the International Space Station.

Then there is Jeff Bezos, who founded Amazon.com and has created the Blue Origin Corporation in Texas. This company is now developing new rocket engines to replace the Russian motors in the Atlas 5 rocket. And Robert Bigelow, who made his billions from the Budget Suites hotel chain, has founded Bigelow Aerospace. This company, under Bigelow's leadership, is intent on developing space habitats that are larger than the International Space Station and a whole lot cheaper in cost. Already he has placed two Genesis "inflatable" spacehabs in orbit. It is possible to go on-line and see the video transmissions that come from these private space station and Bigelow's ultimate plans are for commercial hotels in space. Then there is the computer game developer John Carmack. He is famous and enormously rich for his exploits in developing the computer games "Quake" and "Doom". He has founded Armadillo Aerospace to join the squadron of space billionaires vying to commercialize space transportation and a variety of new space businesses.

Arthur would have been enormously proud to see this all happen. The actuality is a far cry from the PanAm spaceships that were depicted in *2001: A Space Odyssey* but the idea that space systems could make the transition from NASA and space agency experimentation to someday becoming a routine commercial business open to all who wished to travel into the cosmos was very much one of Arthur C. Clarke's heartfelt hopes and aspirations. For those who wish to know more about the space billionaires, their stories can be found in the book *Launching into Commercial Space (2013).*

Future Space Transportation Systems

Commercial space planes are going to be a reality very, very soon. But what about the longer-term future of space transportation systems? Here is where Arthur thrived and absolutely bubbled with a number of exciting new ideas. He was fond of using two of the most logical ways to propel spacecraft from point A to point B in his science fiction stories. One means was to use the gravity well of the Sun or Jupiter to serve as a propulsive force to slingshot forward a spacecraft to exceptionally high speeds. In *Rendezvous with Rama*, the Sun's gravitational well was used to accelerate this mysterious ship in its onward journey. In this case Rama was cleverly equipped with thermal shields to protect it from the Sun's heat as it cruised close to this hot nuclear furnace. In *2010: Odyssey Two* the gravity well of Jupiter served as a slingshot to go on to Saturn.

In *Foundations of Paradise* Arthur indicated in some detail how a space elevator might be deployed to provide large scale and low cost transport out to the geosynchronous orbit. In *3001: The Final Space Odyssey* he invoked his poetic license and imaginative brain to explain how a mysterious positronic drive--much like anti-gravity--would allow not only the creation of a space elevator, but the creation of a series of massive towers that reached from Earth to Geosynchronous orbit. A thousand years in the future Clarke imagined a world where humanity now lived in these massive towers that stretched some 36,000 kilometers up into the cosmos and Earth's surface was a gigantic game park.

The second way Clarke envisioned navigating around the solar system appears in several other of his stories. This was to "use the power of the sun" to create a starship fusion drive that over time can reach near the speed of light. In the short story "The Songs of Distant Earth" written in 1958 this nuclear fusion drive mechanism was described as a way for starships to buildup speeds above 90% of the speed of light and do so even for a massive space ship. Clarke anticipated the major physics problem of particles and micrometeorites encountering a starship at relativistic speeds and the explosive result. In this story, the starship has a huge gigaton chunk of ice that travels in front of the starship to run interference. In both of these propulsive systems Clarke involves well known technology —gravity and nuclear fusion -- that has been proven to work for countless eons. However, he was always tempted to travel beyond the "known" to explore the "unknown" in both his science fiction and his scientific writings. In this case he speculated on technology that had often been envisioned by human thought but never yet achieved in actual fact—at least on planet Earth.

Clarke was a great admirer of Konstantin Tsiolkovsky. He had particularly great enthusiasm for one of his ideas that this great Russian thinker discussed in his published works in 1895 (i.e. "Speculations about Earth and Sky and on Vesta.") The concept relies once again on the magical geosynchronous orbit where everything is in equilibrium. Cargo can be "lifted" most of the way out of the "Earth's gravity well" by creating a space elevator that extends from a terminal spot on the equator all the way out to geosynchronous orbit and beyond where the cable connects to a counterweight that acts as "negative gravity". Any mass beyond Geo and connected to a "space station" in the Clarke orbit actually acts to pull mass out and away from the Earth's surface. And presto there you have it -- negative gravity. This magical effect I believe is why Arthur C. Clarke throughout his career kept coming back to the concept of anti-gravity and the possible future "modulation" of graviton in the space-time continuum.

In writing about these three ways to engage in space transport — gravitational slingshot assist, nuclear fusion star drives, and the space elevator--Clarke actually did not have to conceive any new or undiscovered physics to support the scientific premises in his writings. One might quibble about this conclusion in terms of the advanced material needed for the cable for the space elevator since this cable in the sky needed to be over 40,000 kilometer long (and in some concepts nearly 70,000). Such a super long tethered cable would need to have gigantic tensile strength—like that of diamond. But today nanotube structures, known as Bucky balls in honor of R. Buckminster Fuller, could perhaps do the trick. This advanced carbon structure when in ultimate industrial production could likely meet this very stringent requirement. Also solar-powered climber robots can now be seen as extensions of today's robotic and quantum dot solar power technology. And then there is the concept of a cable that might be designed to connect the Earth and the Moon. This project, oddly enough, could be designed to require a cable that had less tensile strength than the space elevator to geosynchronous orbit. This is because the Earth to Moon and Moon to Earth links would anchor each other in a dynamic rotational system.

These three types of space transport systems that Clarke discussed in his works of fact and fiction represented different levels of technological challenge.

Gravitational Slingshots.   Today the slingshot effect of gravitational fields is demonstrably old hat. This is straight forward dynamic physics that has been demonstrated a number of times in actual space missions—notably the Voyager 1 mission to Jupiter, Saturn, Neptune, Uranus and out of the solar system, and then with the Ulysses mission that went to Jupiter and then back to study the polar regions of the Sun.

Nuclear Fusion Based Propulsion. Researchers of nuclear fusion and magnetically-contained plasma fields claim that they will be able to sustain fusion power sources for longer than a micro-second within a decade. The Arthur C. Clarke Center on the Human Imagination (ACCCHI) Starship Century symposium in 2013 concluded that starship travel using this power source is a reasonable technical expectation within the course of a century—or hopefully less.

Space Elevators. The space elevator, although a very difficult concept with a great deal of new technology to develop and deploy, does not involve any idea that is not easily revealed by orbital mechanics, robotics engineering, or material science. The biggest ultimate challenge may be to build a cable that can withstand the intensive ionic bombardment that will be encountered as the cable penetrates the Van Allen belts. It is ironic that an Earth to Moon elevator may be easier to construct than an Earth to Geo Orbit.

Gravitational Slingshot Expresses

The Voyager 1 mission that the US launched in 1977 to explore Jupiter actually aped the gravitational slingshot effect described in *2010: Odysssey Two* to allow this spacecraft to go on to Saturn. This maneuver was further used to allow Voyager 1 to fly by Neptune and Uranus. This amazing spacecraft is now headed out to the Oort cloud as it leaves the Solar System. It is indeed the first human spacecraft to leave the Solar System to go out into the cosmos and to leave human reach behind forever. The Voyager 1 mission received an enormous amount of publicity not because of its amazing science but for another much more mundane reason entirely. Carl and Linda Sagan and Eric Burgess designed a plaque that showed that this spacecraft came from Earth and was the product of humans. This was done by showing Earth as the third planet from the Sun and then showing the Sun's relationship to some 17 quasars.

This, however, was not what generated the controversy. It was   the depiction of a naked man and woman scaled to the size of the spacecraft. These nude humans displayed not only a upraised palm in a sign of peace but also their male and female genitalia. The "religious right" considered this message as no better than sending pornography to the stars.

In a much less controversial program, the 1990 Ulysses spacecraft used this same type of gravitational slingshot maneuver to change the orbit of this solar exploration mission so that the spacecraft could fly over the unexplored polar regions of the sun. Any "gravitational well" in the space-time continuum can be used to gain some additional velocity but the more massive the planetary or solar object the more velocity advantage that can be achieved. One could even use the gravity of the Moon to accelerate a mission to Mars, but this would be far from the optimum maneuver.

Nuclear Fusion Power Spacecraft

It is well established that the gravitational and magnetic fields of the Sun and the heat that this process generates allows the sun's nuclear furnace to generate enormous amounts of energy on which the Earth's survival depends. Thus the idea of fusion-powered starship makes it appearance in a number of Clarke's stories and novels. In _The Songs of Distant Earth_ (1957) Clarke describes the vast starship Magellan that is driven the "power of the stars". In this story the spaceship has to stop at a distant colony named Thalassa, not to refuel its fusion reactors, but to rebuild a vast protective cosmic umbrella of ice that protects the starship from bits of molecules it encounters in its flight. Since the starship eventually builds up speed to 90% of the speed of light even encounters with tiny bits of matter involve great explosive force. Just like in _2001: A Space Odyssey,_ written a decade later, Clarke describes a vast starship powered by nuclear fusion, controlled by a giant computer while the crew and passengers are asleep in suspended animation. In _The Songs of Distant Earth_ story hundreds of Earth years go by as the star ship travels light years of distance. But in this story only a few months expire for the star travelers because of the incredible relativistic speeds they attain. Clarke does not seek to address what happens to human cells as people are accelerated to near light speeds and thus each person becomes almost infinitely massive. Although we still seem to be some time away from being able to sustain a practical and sustained fusion process, the scientific principles are broadly accepted. It is thus only the space elevator, or more likely the space funicular (A device that would move one carriage upward while the return carriage is moving downward) that remains to be demonstrated in a way that seems close to be feasibility in terms of precise engineering feasibility NASA is currently sponsoring competitive contests that would possibly allow the future construction of such a space tether built by robotic climbers powered by solar energy. As noted earlier, NASA engineers confess that the ionic bombardment to the space elevator as it goes through the Van Allen belts may ultimately prove to be the show stopper in realizing a truly long-lived functional space elevator.

Figure 13.2: Conceptual Image of a Space Elevator
(Graphic Courtesy of NASA)

The image above is a recent conceptualizations for the design of a space elevator . But Clarke's journey into unknown went well beyond the exotic knowledge of the space elevator. He has suggested, consistent with the Clarke Second Law of sufficiently advanced technology being indistinguishable from magic, that anything that anything we can imagine can be invented. He even suggested that with the current exponential rate of technical innovation that virtually everything can now be achieved within the next three hundred years. He leapt from this very arguable premise to the prediction in 2095 that we would invent a totally new concept of interstellar transportation that was based on the development of a true "space drive" - a propulsion system reacting against the structure of space time -that makes the rocket obsolete. What this meant is actually somewhat mysterious and was not clearly distinguished from what he also described as "anti-gravity" transportation systems.

Anti-Gravitational Systems that Exploit Inconsistencies of the Space-Time Continuum

It is with such concepts that Clarke jumped into the most remote distances of the unrealized future.In returning to his short story "The Songs of Distant Earth" (1957) he actually did refer to "anti-gravity scooters". In his _3001: The Final Odyssey_ he refers to a positronic drive that moved up and down space towers that reached from Planet Earth all the way to the geosynchronous orbit in a fashion that also seemed to be a sort of anti-gravity system.

But it was never made clear from a technical or scientific perspective what was meant by the a space drive that "reacted against the structure of space-time" and to what extent this was the same or different from "anti-gravity." What we do know is that he made a series of predictions related to positronic space drives within space towers that extended from Earth to geosynchronous orbit, about anti-gravitational space propulsion systems, and systems that provide transport across space by reacting "against the space-time continuum without clearly distinguishing between these concepts. Since he predicted these capabilities to occur some 80 to

85 years from now, the only real was to uncover the validity of these rather awe inspiring predictions would be to stick around and find out.

Conclusions

Clarke thus envisioned a broad and intriguing range of future transport systems. These included space planes that could fly to orbit and beyond, space elevators to geosynchronous orbit, nuclear drive for interstellar space ships, anti-gravity transport systems, and the use of the gravity wells of the sun and the planets as accelerators. One of the more fascinating aspects of Arthur's writing is that he wrote about subjects involving known engineering and science in books of fact with some rigor, and here rocketry was one of his favorite subjects. When he let his imagination roam into the world of tomorrow then he often shifted gears and sprinkled his books of science fiction with concepts and ideas that might be realized in future years, decades, centuries or even a millennium or two hence. Clarke spent a great deal of his time pondering both the future of sustainable energy and new and advanced transportation systems because both subjects intrigued him and because he saw them so closely interrelated.

Chapter 14

Free and Abundant Power

"If, as is perfectly possible, we are short of energy two generations from now, it will be through our own incompetence...For most of or raw materials, as for our power sources, we have been living on borrowed capital. We have been exploiting the easily available resources—the high grade ores, the rich lodes where natural forces have concentrated the metals and minerals we need. These processes took a billion years or more; in mere centuries, we have looted treasures stored up over aeons. When they are gone, our civilization cannot mark time for a few hundred million years until they are restored. That means we'll have to go back to the original source, the sun." **Arthur C. Clarke, "Profiles of the Future", (1962).**

"The first Quantum Generators (tapping space energy) are developed. Available in portable and household units from a few kilowatts upward, they can produce electricity indefinitely. Central power stations close down; the age of pylons ends as grid systems are dismantled." **Arthur C. Clarke, The 21st Century Beyond 2000, Asia Now".**

"In one [human]lifetime they[automobiles] have consumed more irreplaceable fuel than has been used in the whole previous history of mankind. The roads to support them....cost as much as a small war." **Arthur C. Clarke, "Profiles of the Future", (1962).**

"The heavy hydrogen in the seas can drive all our machines, heat all our cities, for as far ahead as we can imagine." **Arthur C. Clarke, "Profiles of the Future", (1962).**

"Plasmas conduct electricity far better than any metals, and their manipulation by magnetic fields is the basis of the important new science of magnetohydrodynamic—usually for obvious reasons referred to as MDH......Tapping the Sun may sound a fantastic conception, but we are already probing its atmosphere with radio beams. Perhaps one day we may be able to release or trigger the titanic forces at work there." **Arthur C. Clarke, *"Profiles of the Future"*, (1962).**

During the last few decade of Arthur C. Clarke's life, before his death in 2008, he largely focused his enormous brain on the subject of energy, because he considered the issue of "green energy" and sustainability of life on Planet Earth to be closely interrelated. The fact that we were using up valuable resources that had taken over a billion years to form was a particular worry, because he recognized that these energy and material resources could not be easily replaced. Our "pricing concepts" in current economic theory based just on the cost of mining and bringing to market rather than in terms of cost of replacement was both wrong minded and in the longer term quite dangerous.

He also recognized that these same wrong-minded concepts of "economic efficiency" would bring other unintended consequences. The most serious of these we are only beginning to recognize, perhaps much too late. This is the challenge of climate change and the exponential increase in greenhouse gases (GHGs) that comes from always using the cheapest and most available fuel. This strategy, if it continues for just a few decades more and is accompanied by continued population explosion that truly brings human population to the level of 10 to 12 billion, could come to represent an overwhelming threat to human survival.

Climate Change, Over Consumption, and Clean Energy

Clarke was also well aware of cosmic hazards such as asteroids, comets, coronal mass ejections, and severe space weather, but he correctly surmised that the greatest cosmic threat may well eventually be climate change and a sufficient global supply of water to an ever burgeoning global population. As we humans zoom through space around the sun at 67,000 miles per hour (or 107,000 kilometers per hour) and as the sun traverses the Galaxy at 450,000 miles per hour (or 720,000 kilometer per hour) the reality of the Earth's role as a cosmic spaceship cannot be denied. On a real spaceship one would not eat up all the food, drink all the water and use up all the energy supplies without thought as to how these key resources would be resupplied, but this is exactly what Clarke feared we were doing on Spaceship Earth.

This six sextillion ton spaceship does not need to have a propulsion system since the gravitational forces of the space-time continuum keeps Earth on its cosmic track. But Earth does need a protective shield against the cosmic hazards that inhabit free space. Asteroids, comets, solar flares, coronal mass ejections, hyper-energetic cosmic rays and anti-matter all constitute threats to human survival. The Earth's atmosphere, ozone layer and Van Allen belts provide a protective shield that does provide an effective barrier against most of the hazards. The Earth's protective shield is not static nor its long term performance guaranteed. Elements of concern include the changing deflective force of the Van Allen Belts, changes to the geomagnetosphere, the weakening protective ozone layer just above the stratosphere, especially in the polar region, and current GHG build-up in the atmosphere that can lead to intensive overheating. The increasing global population coupled with ever greater volume of carbon-based fuels being burnt in the fragile atmosphere puts spaceship Earth at risk of more violent storms, changing rain patterns, sustained droughts, massive flooding, and dangerous overheating.

The bottom line is that energy—and access to clean and plentiful energy in particular—is critical to the long term viability and resilience of planet

Earth. We need to recognize—as Arthur C. Clarke clearly did—that we are all aboard a very large and complex spaceship Earth. Today, on our spaceship we really have just two assets to draw on. These are a finite stash of Earth-based resources and the Sun. These are what allows humans and all flora and fauna to continue on our journey through the cosmos. If we do not look to developing recyclable and sustainable supplies of resources and limiting population growth we are in for big time problems. Clarke did not explicitly say so, but he really did tend to think that during the 20th century our Space Ship Earth had been taken over by loonies who thought that economic expansion and ever more rapid throughput was more important than anything—even survival. These unlimited economic expansionists seemed to think that Space Ship Earth had unlimited stores of supplies to use up to support endless growth and consumption. It was his hope that in the 21st century a new cadre of Earth Ship Commanders would say "WHOA!"

Survival of our spaceship stores and preservation of the species is now the top priority. Let's begin a systematic focus on resiliency, recycling of resources and controlling unreasonable growth that could lead to runaway climate change and permanent damage to our spaceship-- to the extent that it can no longer sustain life or at least not the human kind. The 2014 report of the World Wildlife Foundation made two very profound observations. One conclusion was that human activity has now managed to kill off about half of vertebrate animals on Planet Earth. The second conclusion is that there would need to be 1.5 Earths to sustain current levels of consumption of energy and resources and the disparity between resources and consumption is increasing each year.

Ultimately it was this fear in Arthur's mind, as clearly noted in the quotation provided at the start of this chapter, that has been re-echoing in the words of scientists and commentators such as Stephen Hawking, Carl Sagan, Neil deGrasse Tyson, Peter Diamandis and others. They –like Clarke before them-- see space exploration as not just the pursuit of knowledge, but as a way to provide a life raft for humanity if we ultimately find that life on Space Ship Earth is doomed. Hawking has been more explicit about his concerns, because Clarke never wished to be an alarmist, but his social concerns in this regard were strong. I do believe that Arthur would have agreed with the following statements by British Astrophysicist Hawking when he said: *""Life on Earth is at the ever-increasing risk of being wiped out by a disaster such as sudden global warming, nuclear war, a genetically engineered virus or other dangers ... I think the human race has no future if it doesn't go into space..........I don't think the human race will survive the next 1,000 years unless we spread into space.... The earth is **the cradle** of humankind, but one cannot live in **the cradle** forever."*

Figure 14.1: Spaceship Earth Has a Fragile Atmosphere and Limited Resources

Arthur Clarke understood the finiteness of the world. This is why he spent a good deal of time exploring the feasibility of sea mining to obtain resources once humans had expended the resources available on land. He even questioned why we call our planet Earth when so much of the terrain is covered by sea water? His candidate name was indeed "Ocean". What Clarke understood quite clearly is that hydrocarbon fuels such as coal and oil would be at best a transitory fuel for humans and that it was a very dirty energy source at that. In other words consumption of these dirty energy sources was bad for our health in terms of air and water pollution, bad because it generated greenhouse gases (GHG) that lead to climate change and global warming, and bad because we are going to run out of these scarce resource in any event. For this wasteful usage he faulted automobiles, but he could have also faulted our consumption for heating, electricity generation, and other profligate uses as well. He suggested that we should conserve petroleum as a way to grow food for a burgeoning world population.

You can put some microbes in a test tube with sugar and water and bread and the microbes will multiply and thrive like gang busters. A few microbes will expand to millions with no trouble at all until all the bread and sugar are gone and then there is almost instantaneous extinction. We humans tend to think we are smarter than microbes.

But then we tried an experiment called Biosphere II in a large complex in Arizona in the United States. The results were ultimately disastrous.

The bio-spherians were locked inside of a large sealed building that included the ability to grow crops, experience rain and condensation, and carry out human enterprise. The experiment was to see if humans could create a stable and sustainable life environment for an extended period of time. The answer was no! There was a need to vent carbon dioxide gas after a few months. Otherwise those inside Biosphere II would have surely died. We did better than the microbes but not by a whole lot. The end result was the same. We cannot create a stable and sustainable environment.

Figure 14.2: Biosphere 2: The Failed Experiment in Human Sustainability

The International Space Station is highly dependent on the delivery of fresh supplies and discarding waste into departing spacecraft. The recycled water and air is just one of the problems with trying to create a self-sustaining human space station or colony in space. Of all the problems related to long term sustainability of human society, Arthur C. Clarke recognized—well before Biosphere II—the need to create sustainable energy sources. He devoted much of the final stages of his life to identifying new energy sources that were clean and green. He clearly saw that current uses of coal, oil, jet fuel and gasoline (particularly leaded gasoline) were polluting the atmosphere, creating toxic environments and would lead to a terminal result for humans and all wild life if continued indefinitely.

Today there is legitimate concern about climate change, GHG build up, limited potable water supplies, and global warming. But there are other concerns as well. Aircraft flights into the stratosphere are weakening the ozone layer that protects us from cosmic rays, X-rays and ultra-violet radiation that can and does lead to sunburn, genetic mutations and cancer. As Clarke understood, the burgeoning population of humanity leads to environmental changes that could in time be fatal to humans and even most animal and vegetative life. His concerns in this regard had many points of origin. These included the incredible consumption of oil and gasoline within the span of his own lifetime which exceeded by a large margin the entirety of the consumption that had occurred in the millions of years that had come before. It was in considering how humans could survive for the longer term future that led him to concentrate on clean energy. Ultimately this ended with him trying to envision how to create sustainable starships that could take humanity to new planetary homes light years away.

Any person who tries to think long term must come to grips with resiliency, sustainability and recyclable energy. In the end this comes to energy that comes directly or indirectly from the stars. Arthur C. Clarke was in this regard no exception. In his research, he monitored contemporaneous clean energy systems that were currently being developed around the world in such areas as solar cells, wind turbines, magnetohydrodynamics (MDH), advanced batteries and fuel cells. His vision was truly focused on breakthrough concepts such as fusion enabled by heavy hydrogen fuels or concepts like Ocean Thermal Energy Conversion (OTEC) that particularly resonated with him because he saw a special connection with his adopted home of Sri Lanka.

The Oracle of Colombo spent much of the last two decades of his life trying to find creditable new clean, green and recyclable energy. He was particularly distracted by the "cold fusion" controversy that erupted in 1989 with its quirky offer of a seemingly short cut to a fabulous fortune of fusion-based futures. As always, Arthur was intrigued by the mysterious, the exotic, and the promise of an unexpected bonanza. Let's review some of his energy speculations.

Ocean Thermal Energy Conversion (OTEC)

After he completed his university studies in the UK in 1948, Arthur C. Clarke spent the next few years trying to explore the seas. Trips to Florida in the U.S., the Great Barrier Reef in Australia, and the seas around Sri Lanka were scuba diving paradises. He not only made his second home in Sri Lanka, but actually went into the scuba diving business with his partner Hector. On the commercial road next to his home at 5 Barnes Place, Colombo, window displays announced the exotic capabilities of Underwater Safaris. If you think about the oceans and Clarke's infatuation with outer space, it is not hard to comprehend his thought process that concluded with the following: "If I will never go into outer space, then the oceans are the closest that I will ever come to transiting a completely foreign and phantasmagorical world."

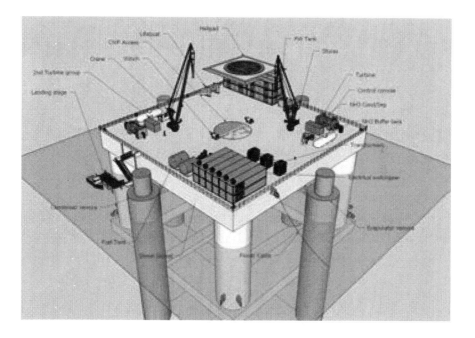

Figure 14.3: An Ocean Thermal Energy Conversion Plant

But beyond loving the oceans and the beauties they offered, Clarke also saw the seas as a source of energy that was clean, green and quite accessible with the right new technology. Always at the ready with a phrase that could capture the human imagination, he introduced me to the idea of how the oceans could supply energy to the world when we played table tennis in the afternoon. I commented on the current energy crises that beset the world and he replied crisply: "OTEC is the answer to OPEC".

He went on to explain how the temperature differentials in the ocean were a great and recurring source of energy that humans should be exploiting. Arthur only had to go to his place of business to show how Ocean Thermal Energy Conversion could work. First we know that energy extremes can generate energy and that thermocouples can use temperature differentials to produce electricity. Neil Ruzik's patent is on record with the US Patent Office to use the huge temperature change from the sunlit surface of the moon and its nearby dark side in order to allow a large-scale thermocouple to provide electricity to a lunar colony. In the case of OTEC the idea is use the heat of the sun to warm water at the surface and cold of the ocean depths to use heat cycles to break down ocean water into hydrogen and oxygen. In one concept the hydrogen is then cooled and then shipped around the world as liquid hydrogen fuel. This all purpose fuel could be used to create heat at power plants or could be used to power cars or planes. These power plants and vehicles of the future would not expel noxious hydrocarbon greenhouse gases (GHGs) but simply expel water vapor.   As long as the Sun and the oceans are there this cycle can go on forever. This is one technology that has evolved slowly, but several experimental OTEP plants exist at places like Hawaii. Unfortunately, there are none in Sri Lanka as Arthur C. Clarke had hoped. Today this process is not considered economic, and there is no distribution system to effectively use liquid hydrogen. However, in future decades this technology could become an important recyclable energy source as the cost of oil continues to climb.

Heavy Hydrogen—Mined from the Seas

Another energy source from the oceans that Clarke felt could become important would involve the future mining of heavy hydrogen from the oceans. He saw tremendous potential in mining the seas for many minerals and resources, but he saw heavy hydrogen as a particularly valuable resource. "The heavy hydrogen in the seas can drive all our machines, heat all our cities, for as far ahead as we can imagine."

Clarke's reference to heavy hydrogen is actually a reference what is scientifically known as deuterium. Deuterium is an isotope of hydrogen that is found in large quantities in water—including ocean water. There is about one atom per ten thousand hydrogen atoms that has a deuterium nucleus. This relatively stable isotope is denoted "2H" or "D", and is used in a number of conventional nuclear reactors in the form of heavy water (D_2O). The real potential for future energy production could be its use in future nuclear fusion reactors as opposed to today's dangerous nuclear fission reactors.

Initial experiments have tried use to iced or super cooled deuterium as a dense nuclear fusion fuel, but with limited results. The current research is now aimed at converting iced deuterium into something called "ultra-dense deuterium" or what is sometimes called "metallic hydrogen". This material is a million times more dense than even super-cooled hydrogen. Scientists believe this material could be used as a fuel for nuclear fusion to warm our cities or even be employed as the fusion drive for starships of the future. The material with its nuclei smashed together would be so dense that a baseball sized chunk of it would weigh about 100 metric tons. Impacted by very high intensity lasers and contained by magnetic forces it could supply not only enormous energy, but perhaps even more significantly, it would produce clean byproducts—namely hydrogen and helium. Thus there would be no radioactive waste to contaminate the Earth.

There is also research on-going with regard to the possible use of tritium 3H--an even heavier and rarer hydrogen isotope as a fuel source for fusion. So far these experiments have not been successful in producing ultra-dense tritium. The key is that "ultra dense deuterium", which unfortunately has currently only been produced in microscopic amounts in the lab, results in H nuclei being pushed much closer together than any other known material. It is thus thought that starting the fusion process will be much easier to begin and sustain than with any other known substance.

Clarke's challenge of mining the seas will certainly be difficult to achieve in a practical sense since most of the suspended materials in the oceans is low value salt. The greatest challenge of all would be to find a practical way to convert conventional heavy hydrogen to ultra-dense deuterium at reasonable cost. If we can do both things we could in theory solve all our future energy needs and stop the build-up of CO_2. greenhouse gases as well.

"Cold Fusion" -- Low Energy Nuclear Reactions (LENR) and Chemically Assisted Nuclear Reactions (CANR)

Arthur always loved a good mystery, particularly if it involved unsolved scientific disputes. Thus it is not surprising that he was greatly intrigued by the experiments of Professors Stanley Pons and Martin Fleischmann, at the University of Utah in 1989 that became known as the still enigmatic concept of "cold fusion". These experimenters claimed that deuterium and electrolytes interacting with Pallatium metal were somehow able to overcome the coulomb resistance that protects the nuclear integrity of matter. Some 25 years later there is still debate over the phenomena that is now often called Low Energy Nuclear Reactions (LENR) or Chemically Assisted Nuclear Reaction. What is also clear is that the U.S. Patent Office is refusing to issue patents for "inventions" in the "cold fusion" field despite the fact that hundreds of patent applications are now pending.

What is interesting is that there are now at least nine processes involving chemical interactions that seem to give off more energy in terms of heat and so-called "nuclear reactions" than went into the experiment. Regardless of the theoretical explanation a process that seems to produce an increase in net energy without a polluting residue remains of interest.

Not only did   Clarke feel this was a topic worth pursuing, but energy-poor Japan has now invested significantly in research in this field to see if there is truly some magical answer here. Many are willing to write this off as alchemist fraud, but new claims keep coming in about how to achieve low temperature nuclear reaction processes.

Recently a California based company known as E-Quest Sciences has claimed that they can employ high-intensity ultrasonic frequencies rather than lasers to load deuterium into palladium from a heavy water solution and produce a net energy increase. They claim excess heat is produced in this process--along with helium. The scientific world remains skeptical but Arthur's special gift was to accept what conventional wisdom claims to be impossible without being naïve enough in his scientific and world view to seek independent scientific verification. Too often the scientific community has remained stubbornly resistant to new information that rocked the conventional view of reality. If not for brave iconoclasts perhaps we would still think the Sun revolves around the Earth, or have no clue how evolution really works, or think that distant galaxies are just bright stars. Perhaps it will ultimately prove that Low Energy Nuclear Reactions becomes yet another dream of low cost, clean energy dashed. Still Arthur C. Clarke sincerely hoped that this was not an impossible dream and was worthy of further research up until the time he died in 2008.

Conclusions

The hope of Arthur C. Clarke was that we would someday soon find an affordable and clean source of energy from the ocean, the Sun, or fusion. This was most central on his mind before he died. This is because he saw clean and renewable energy as the pathway for long-term human survival. One thing is clear. The Age of Hydro Carbon-Based Energy on Planet Earth will last somewhere between 300 years and 400 years out of its 4.5 billion year history. This "era of oil" has been called "Hubbert's Pimple" by World Bank analysts. This rather disparaging reference is based on a simple historical line drawing showing the "teeny tiny" slot of time that we humans were dependent on hydrocarbons to fuel our society and its transport system. In short, Clarke continually hoped that we would be smart enough to see that oil was a dead end in terms of an ultimately vanishing resource, but also, that in terms of pollution and climate change, it might also be quite literally a "dead end".

Today, the best hope for clean renewable energy seemingly comes from photovoltaic cells and quantum dot technology—the next big thing that may one day replace solar cells. Slowly, over the last 40 years, solar cell-produced power has become a major player. Today, as my friend Peter Varadi, who was a pioneer in this field, notes there is today 100 Giga Watts of already deployed solar cell arrays around the world—the equivalent of 20 nuclear energy power plants. Even more impressively this capability is now growing at 30% per year. Perhaps there is yet still hope for clean and abundant energy and for the survivability of humanity. Clarke would smile to note that at current growth rates, solar cell energy could outstrip oil energy levels in a couple of decades. Let's hope this is soon enough to prevent run away and irreversible global heating.

PART III:

Final Considerations

Chapter 15
When Clarke Got It Wrong

"It may well be that the submarine cable, even in the moment of its greatest technical triumph for a hundred years, is already doomed." **Arthur C. Clarke, "_Voice Across the Sea_", (1957).**

"In his short story "Cosmic Casanova" Arthur C. Clarke hypothesizes that humans that lived for thousands of years in a very low gravity environment such as a small planet would grow much larger in size and become giants." **Arthur C. Clarke in "_The Other Side of the Sky_".**

Questionable or Just Wrong Predictions by **Arthur C. Clarke in "_Profiles of the Future_", (1962):**
- Fusion Power and Cyborgs (Achievable by 1990)
- Time, Perception Enhancements and Wireless Energy (Achievable by 2000)
- Weather Control (Achievable by 2010)
- Interstellar Probes (Achievable by 2020)
- Contact with Extra-Terrestrial (Achievable by 2030)

"For the nemesis of the ocean-going freighter may not be the submarine or the aeroplane, but the Ground Effect Machine, riding on cushions of air over land and sea…..If you are content to float only a few inches from the ground, you can support, for the same horsepower many times the load that a helicopter can lift into the open sky." **Arthur C. Clarke, "_Profiles of the Future_", (1962).**

"What would be ideal is some nice, clean way, probably electrical, of abolishing gravity at the throw of a switch." **Arthur C. Clarke, "_Profiles of the Future_", (1962).**

"What about the City of the Day after Tomorrow, say the year 2000….it may not even exist at all….. the traditional role of the city as a meeting place for man will no longer make sense…..I only hope when the city is abolished the whole world is not converted into one giant suburb." **Arthur C. Clarke, BBC Interview in 1964.**

"Another possibility is that , even if a fourth direction of dimension of [physical] space does not exist in nature , we may be able to create such an extension artificially." **Arthur C. Clarke, "_Profiles of the Future", (1962)._**

As remarkable as Arthur C. Clarke's track record is in predicting the future, there is no such thing as a perfect psychic power of prediction that can forecast the future with unerring accuracy. Only if we are someday able to develop time travel will we be able to predict the future with absolute certainly. Of course, as Clarke has noted, if everything were certain, predetermined and knowable, then life would be incredibly dull. What would be the fun of going to a sporting event if the result was already known?

If we could time travel we would simply go forward and back in time and observe whatever unknown event we were curious about. Of course if everyone could travel to the future things like stock markets would be thrown into utter chaos. It would therefore change the future if everyone knew what stocks would go up or down and then act on it. If one could actually engage in time travel and act on it, it would create an infinite number of futures.

Clarke's remarkably accurate future predictions stem from a variety of sources. His powers of prediction start with his paying close attention to the writings of astute scientists, engineers, authors of science fiction, artists and inventive thinkers of the past who have already had incredible insights. It is amazing that few people do go back and read the writings of

Aristotle, Leonardo, Galileo, Copernicus, Konstantin Tsiokovsky and other greats. Clarke credits a great number of people like Jules Verne, Hermann Noordung, Robert Heinlein, Yuri Artsutanov, Bernoit Mandelbrot and others for many of his ideas and inspiring writings.

Further he was also constantly monitoring the research activities of many people in laboratories, universities, and institutes around the world to keep current on new developments as they were occurring. When I visited Arthur a 5 Barnes Place in Sri Lanka in pre-Internet days, I was struck by the fact that there were hundreds of journals from around the world in his huge office that he not only subscribed to but apparently also read with the thoroughness and interest that was so indicative of his vacuum-cleaner like mind.

Finally, there was the inventive right side of his brain. Arthur had an incredibly rich imagination that was constantly bubbling forth new ideas and clever concepts. These pearls of insight—like the artist that he was--seemed to leap into his mind nearly fully formed. Some people go on various types of binges such as eating, drinking, or shopping, but Arthur C. Clarke went on intellectual binges. Within a single week he might delve into such diverse subjects as space elevators, artificial intelligence, space communications antenna farms, desktop fusion—now more accurately known as Low Energy Nuclear Reactions (LENR), non-linear math and Mandebrot fractals, sea mining, and Ocean Thermal Energy Conversion   He had an uncanny ability to assimilate a huge amount of information into his brain in a very short period of time and then also be able to synthesize this information into his big picture view of the world and the cosmos. He could fit it all together using both the left and   right side of his brain. This is how he could become an expert and visionary across so many fields. In short, he was a very special sort of polymath that is quite rare—someone with the collective capabilities of an Einstein, a systems engineer, a Leonardo, a Shakespeare and an idiot savant. .

It was his capabilities and myriad interests that could allow him so many insights into how things would evolve—particularly in the realm of science and engineering. But this was insight and not some sort of otherworldly séance that would actually reveal the future fully formed. In a word, Arthur C. Clarke could indeed get things wrong and actually did come up with some thoughts about the future that turned out to be a substantial part of a parsec off. His predictions that we would by now have harnessed many new technologies that are still years away from fruition may mean that he was "optimistic" rather than "wrong". Certainly he had anticipated much that we should have by now conquered: fusion power, the control of weather, wireless energy, wireless energy distribution, cyborgs, and Ground Effect Machines (GEMS). These GEMs were transport systems that would float via powerful fan jets over the land and sea. These predictions can certainly seem wide of the mark today. However, one could also write this down to failed human intelligence and engineering.

"Pending" Predictions

In his *Profiles of the Future* he rather daringly made a wide range of predictions as to when many new technologies and capabilities would be achieved. If one tallies the prediction up, more of them have come true than not.   There are many "still pending predictions" for later in the 21st century that could have a plausible chance of still being realized -- although perhaps some decades past where he said they might come true. Clearly he was overly optimistic about our being able to sustain a consistent nuclear fusion process of more than a nanosecond. Certainly cyborgs are still a ways downstream. The projected times for Perception Enhancements (2000), Wireless Energy (2000). Weather Control (2010) and Interstellar Probes (2020) have come and gone. We can write off 2020 interstellar probes because we currently have no propulsion technology that could sustain such a mission today and certainly it would take at least five years to fund and build such a spacecraft. Certainly it would not be valid to count the Voyager as such a spacecraft in that this vehicle is way too slow to reach any star system any century soon (Voyager I has not even reach the Oort cloud nearly 40 years after its launch) and even if it did reach another star system it would not be able to send back any information that could be received.

The most unlikely of all of all of Clarke's nearer term predictions at this point seems to be contact with extraterrestrial intelligence by 2030. This skepticism is based on a half century of zero success in this department and the fact that we have no very good idea as to which media another intelligence might use to communicate—quasars, X- rays, cosmic rays, etc.

Another of his predictions that has not only turned out to be wrong, but has actually moved in the opposite direction is the "evaporation" of the city. Clarke correctly anticipated the advent of telecommuting, tele-education, and tele-health services that has been spurred by the capabilities that satellites, fiber and coaxial networks, wi-fi and wireless cellular systems have brought to the world. The broadband capabilities have brought key services to rural and remote areas where schools and doctors are scarce. This capability has indeed made it possible for professionals to reside wherever they choose and working remotely using telecommunications networks. We now call these individuals "lone eagles" and I even have friends in Colorado that answer to this description. Even what I have called "electronic immigrants" in my book "e-Sphere: The Rise of the Worldwide Mind" now exist. Indeed these people that live in one country and work in another number in the millions. Computer programmers in South Korea or Russia can support companies in Europe.

Call centers linked to businesses world-wide are staffed by shift workers in India. The back offices of Wall Street in New York City are actually located in Ireland. Clarke thought that if communications could free workers to live where they wished and link to their offices via telecommunications the role of the city would diminish. But cities have actually grown—and enormously so.

What Clarke did not envisage was the continuing increase in global population from about 4.5 billion people—the time when he made this forecast in 1962-- to over 7 billion today. And this surge has largely come in the developing world. What we have seen is the world going from about 40% urban in 1964 to 53% urban today. Further by 2050 the world may have a global population of 8.5 billion and risen to be 70% urban. Massive urban centers have grown up across much of the world. Megacities are sprouting everywhere, and certainly are not disappearing.

Figure 15.1: High-rise Urban Centers, not Shrinking but Growing World-Wide

This continuing surge of growth in cities is fueled by people moving to these urban areas to find jobs. Countries like Nigeria, which is now projected to overtake the population of the U.S. and thus become the world's third largest country, is currently growing at nearly 7% per annum. Lagos may grow to 40 million people with a huge percentage of these people—mostly young people--seeking jobs in vast megacities with runaway growth. Even in highly developed economies sprawling urban centers (a mass of urbs, suburbs, and ex-urbs) are growing rapidly as we see megacities of more than 10 million people sprouting almost everywhere around the world. China alone already has more than a dozen megacities. Arthur C. Clarke's vision in 1964 was of an increasingly rational and structured world with an interconnected global service economy that allowed people to live and work where they pleased. Unfortunately this vision has been overtaken by a much more "irrational world" with over population, a lack of jobs created by super automation on one hand and a surfeit of new young people on the other.

Figure 15.2: Urban Futures in an Over Populated World?

This has also led to an over consumption of resources and a spike in energy usage. This has been primarily driven by ever increasing use of hydrocarbon-based fuels which has also led to climate change, ocean and atmospheric pollution, and global warming. Perhaps this was the one case where Arthur Clarke's predictions were driven by desire for "what should be" versus a prediction of "what is to be" in our world that is increasingly growing out of control.

Arthur also predicted large-scale use of birth control and DNA testing to control disease. These are technologies that if applied more systematically might have led more in the direction that Clarke predicted in 1964.

The Function of Utopian and Dystopian Science Fiction and Futurism in Modern Society

The world of futurists as well as science fiction writers is essentially divided into two camps. There are those who are generally utopian—i.e. those who see the future as unfolding in a positive way. Then there are their counterparts, the dystopian writers. They foresee the future as generally descending into chaos, warfare or evil. At the very least they depict a world of decline and lowered expectations. Many of these writers from the 18th century, such as Jonathan Swift with his _Gulliver's Travels_, Samuel Butler in his _Erewhon_ to H. G. Wells in _The Time Machine,_ often wrote dystopian literature not so much as a prediction but as a satirical comment about human political and social conditions of their times—perhaps motivated by a desire to provide a caution as to that which should be avoided.

Dystopian science fiction and predicted negative futures from the 20th Century has been different in that it harbors true fears of a more negative future often resulting from concerns about new telecommunications, computer, electronics, bioengineering and artificial intelligence. The most famous of these dystopian books include George Orwell's _1984_, Aldous Huxley's _A Brave New World_, Kurt Vonnegut Jr.'s _Player Piano_, Ray Bradbury's _Fahrenheit 451_, Anthony Burgess' _A Clockwork Orange,_ and more recently William Gibson's _Neuromancer,_ Margaret Atwood's _Cat's Eye,_ Robin Cook's _Coma,_ and Neal Stephenson's _Quicksilver_.

These writers, who often characterize themselves as "speculative fiction" writers usually explain that they are not predicting the future, but merely exposing possible futures. They usually add that their literature does provide a warning against a future that might be. They also explain that it has been well documented that most forecasts and predictions contain a positive bias. Research has, for instance, consistently shown that "smokers" consistently believe they are less likely to contract cancer than actual statistics show. Business forecasts tend to be 70% to 75% positive rather than being half and half in their assessment. Downturns in the stock market are less anticipated than assumed upturns.

But Arthur C. Clarke does not fall comfortably into the category of utopian or dystopian writer. He truly sought to understand what technological paths forwards are being pursued and those most likely to bear fruit. With equal fervor he also assessed where technology and social and economic trends could well lead us into future trouble. It was his fervent believe that solving the "clean and green energy puzzle" was the greatest and most important challenge of modern times. It is true that one can find dozens of Arthur C. Clarke's predictions that have not come to fruition. But it is equally true that this batting average was very likely above 50% especially with regard to significant predictions related to satellites, telecommunications, information technology, networking, energy, artificial intelligence, and space exploration and applications.

He was neither a wild-eyed optimist nor a pessimistic dystopian. His strong suit was tough-minded logic that evaluated technological trends, societal and economic constraints, and past precedents. More than any other, however, he did not look to the future through a rear view mirror but a special crystal that provided truly remarkable insight. He very consistently looked at both the positive and negative potential of technology in making his predictions. He tried to put aside his bias as to what should be. Rather he tried to probe, first and foremost, what most likely will actually occur.

Conclusions

After he reached a conclusion about a new technology or human capability or crafted yet another a prediction Arthur C. Clarke assessed the degree to which this might be a good or bad thing for global society. He often thought outside the box. After he had done so, it was then that he tried to help us consider what we should try to "put back in the box" for the good of humanity. As a realist he intuitively knew that human innovation was essentially a one-way process with a gate that once opened does not close again.

Ultimately it is not important that Arthur may have missed some predictions. His correct insights have pointed us to a future that largely defines our world from the Internet to global communications, from artificial intelligence to instantaneous mobile communications, from electronic banking to GPS navigation and "driverless cars".

Clarke developed a way of visualizing the future that was able to leap ahead not a year or two, but could envision innovations that were 20, 30, 50 or even hundreds of years ahead. His most profound prediction may well turn out to be his forecast that virtually all technical innovations we can now conceive of might be achieved in the next 300 years. If one considers where human technology was in 1800 and where it is today and then adjust for accelerating rates of human progress, this may just turn out to be entirely on track.

Chapter 16

Why Is Arthur C. Clarke Still Relevant?

"One of the technologies that I worry a great deal about is that of creating a huge electromagnetic pulse. One can develop the capability to generate an enormous EMP that could fry all the electronics for 300 miles that would totally disable most countries. We cannot all live inside of Faraday cages." **Arthur C. Clarke, Interview with Internet Society Representatives, 2002.**

"The creation of wealth is certainly not to be despised, but in the long run the only human activities really worthwhile are the search for knowledge, and the creation of beauty. This is beyond argument; the only point of debate is which comes first."– **"Quotes of Arthur C. Clarke" - The Clarke Institute for Science Education.**

"It may be the greatest virtue of the ultra-intelligent machine that it will force us to think about the purpose and meaning of human existence." **"The Odyssey of a Visionary" - biography of Arthur C. Clarke (2013)**

".....ours may be a Golden Age, compared with the endless vista of famine and poverty that must follow when the billions of the future must fight over Earth's waning resources. If this is true then it is all the more vital that we establish self-sustaining colonies on the planets." **Arthur C. Clarke, "Profiles of the Future", (1962).**

"It has yet to be proven that intelligence has any survival value." - **"Quotes of Arthur C. Clarke" - the Clarke Institute for Science Education.**

There are many individuals that have their fifteen minutes of fame and then fade from the limelight. Pop singers, movie stars, and political officials burn brightly across the media, until they are replaced by the latest media darling to make a new movie, issue a commanding sound bite, sign a new bill into law, or show some skin or engage in a peccadillo. Only a special few hold a special place in history that make them timeless icons that will be remembered through the ages. Arthur C. Clarke has enormous staying power for many reasons. His amazing predictions, his compelling science fiction stories and movies, his contributions to the development of satellites, space travel, radar, new energy systems and information technology are all worthy of special remembrance, but these are all things that can fade from memory over time.

What most contributes to Arthur C. Clarke's status as a 20th century icon is his ability to think timeless thoughts at the very core and essence of a human's future. Will we solve our energy and overpopulation problems before we become a failed experiment? Will rampant capitalism destroy the potential for *homo sapiens* survival on Earth and force us to colonize other planets? Will we as a species recognize the enormous destructive force of cosmic hazards in time to create the technology needed to defend Planet Earth against a huge strike by an asteroid or comet or a severe solar event? Will climate disruptions that ultimately transform Earth into an inferno like Venus or erosion of the ozone layer and shifts in the Van Allen belt lead to uncontrolled mutations that prevent the long term survival of the human race? Will intelligent beings in the form of cyborgs, smart robots, replicants, or bio-engineered brain systems replace humans as the "dominant force" on Planet Earth? What is the purpose and reason for the existence of intelligent life? Are humans and intelligent life the anti-entrophic force in the universe? Is the purpose of human existence to create knowledge and beauty and in the process overcome entropy?

What is the longer-term purpose and goals of humanity after we create thinking machines that are smarter than humans and can perform all necessary work?

Not since the days of Plato and Socrates has a central philosophical figure, with the ability to speak clearly to mass audiences, been able to raise such profound questions and probe the meaning of human existence. It is this core capability that makes Arthur C. Clarke a philosophic maven for the ages. There are literally dozens of themes, concepts and technological systems that Clarke explored during his lifetime that could alter the future course of human existence and impact the future potential of *homo sapiens*. The first chart in the appendices provides not only a listing of some of his most important predictions, but also a modest catalogue of industries that in one way or another owe an intellectual debt to Sir Arthur.

This chapter seeks to examine why Arthur C. Clarke relevant is today—and if we survive will make him relevant 300 years hence. In making this case only three basic issues will be explored even though a dozen could be explored and pondered. The three key issues considered are these:

- Are humans smart enough to organize a true planetary "safeguard" to protect Earth from comets, asteroids, cosmic rays. severe space weather and other hazards in our travels through the universe? (In Clarke's novel <u>*Rendezvous with Rama*</u> humans finally get around to doing this in a serious way in 2077.)
  - What is the purpose of human existence? Is there a mission to create knowledge and beauty and is this "The human mission "? Is it the purpose of all intelligent life in the universe, i.e. humanity along with perhaps other alien intelligent life forms, to serve as a counterbalance to entropy? In other words is "intelligence" an especially created natural force to offset the tendency in nature to move to disorder—a sort of antidote to Newton's Second Law?
  - Is the 21st century somehow a very narrow, critical and perilous passageway to the future where climate change, overpopulation and other challenges test whether humans survive or become a failed experiment?

Planetary Defense

The system to detect nuclear explosions in the atmosphere that has been in place since 2001 has detected 26 hits to planet Earth by asteroids that are equivalent to thermonuclear explosions. Fortunately these events have occurred in remote locations and at relatively high altitudes. Yet the odds in favor of a disastrous asteroid strike are not encouraging. The latest data from the NASA NEO WISE Program (i.e. Near Earth Object Wide-range Infrared Surveyor Explorer), from ground observations, and from the atmospheric monitoring program suggest that there are perhaps a million NEOs that are above 30 meters in diameter or larger. This means that there are a million city killer NEOs out there and as human population increases to 10 to 12 billion and urban density increases from current levels of 53% of all people on Earth living in cities to 70%, the chances of a catastrophic hit increases. And a cataclysmic hit by an asteroid or comet is just one cosmic danger.

A major coronal mass ejection that sends billions of ions on a collision course with Planet Earth is an even more likely event. Such a hit could likely take out the electrical grid in many countries and potentially disable many communications, navigation, remote sensing   and weather satellites with enormous impact on global transportation, banking, information networks, and communications. This could have a major impact on supply chains, service jobs and educational and health care systems. Some estimates suggest that a severe enough hit—perhaps increased in effect and impact by shifts in the Earth's magnetic field and a weakening of the Van Allen belts events – could involve trillions of dollars in economic loss and even widespread starvation and massive scales of unemployment that could last a hundred years.

The bottom line is that there are a wide range of potential cosmic hazards that range from space weather and asteroid hits to genetic mutations that could harm vegetation, animals and humans. This is not to mention problems such as orbital debris build up that could threaten safe access to space in the future, run away climate change, or biological contamination from space. Currently the world's nations spend trillions of dollars on military programs to fight other countries and protect their borders, but expenditures and programs to protect Earth from a range of cosmic hazards that could cause much greater devastation and even threaten the survival of the human race is a paltry amount. NASA was assigned the job of surveying the heavens to find all potentially hazardous asteroids down to the size of 140 meters in diameter.

The dismal result is that NASA scientists are almost a decade behind schedule with no program that can effectively complete this task. The saddest fact of all is that asteroids that are over a 100 times less massive, i.e. down to 30 meters in size, still pack the punch of a nuclear bomb and are "city killers". NASA has no program that would accomplish such a detailed cosmic survey. Only a private initiative, as spearheaded by the B612 Foundation, would have a chance of locating the nearly one million city killers out there and help give us a 100 year time horizon warning capability.

And this is just to help identify the possibility of threats. There are scientific and engineering efforts that are designed to deflect asteroids and/or mitigate their impact on Earth but these are today very rudimentary programs. Again private initiatives such as the Planetary Society's program (called the "laser bees" experiment) is proposing the idea of sending small lasers out into space to irradiate NEOs that could possibly hit Earth. The purpose of the laser beams would be to heat up the asteroid so as to create small jets to shoot from the surface of the asteroid and slowly push the asteroid into a new orbit. And when it comes to mitigation programs to protect Earth from severe cosmic weather we are in even worse shape. There are virtually no research efforts at all in place to try to develop protective systems against natural solar weather phenomena such as coronal mass ejections that could generate massive natural ElectroMagnetic Pulses (EMPs).

As we become more and more dependent on electrical energy, information technology and communications in a global service economy the danger of a knockout blow from the Sun becomes more and more likely each year. It is as if we are playing a game of Russian Roulette with the Sun, except that each year there are more bullets in the gun's chamber.

Add to this concern, the added risk that accumulates to modern society by around 2050 when we might have 10 billion people on the planet with 70% of this population living in cities highly dependent on electrical power systems and employment dependent on complex but crucial infrastructures.

As of today only some 500 people have flown into space and seen Earth as it really is. This is a small six sextillion ton mudball that is an insignificant object less than 0.1% of mass of the solar system. It is the hope of those that support the growth of the so-called space tourism business (and perhaps more accurately the space adventures enterprises) that when many thousands of people have flown into space and seen just how vulnerable we are, then we will change our ways and start taking planetary defense seriously.

Few people recognize that our protective atmosphere that we take for granted and pollute with cavalier distain is proportionately less than the skin of an apple. If one had asked Clarke about cosmic hazards and planetary defense, I am sure that he would have said something like: "Maybe it would be a good idea to revise the mission statements for all our space agencies to place planetary defense at the top of their strategic objectives." He also might have said: "You know it is hard to have a space program without any people around to pay the taxes."

Figure 16.1: Spaceship2 with Carrier Plane. This Craft Is Envisioned to Take Many Hundreds of People into Near Earth Space in the Next Few Years (Image from SpaceShip Corporation)

If the human race is to survive with its extreme dependence on modern infrastructure it needs to think less about preparing for and carrying out wars against other members of its species and spend far more understanding cosmic hazards and building a truly viable planetary defense program. This means understanding and cataloguing the risks, developing capabilities to recover from a major cosmic disaster, and ultimately developing the technology to prevent catastrophes from the cosmos actually occurring. Clarke was one of the first to recognize clearly cosmic dangers and one of the very first to rate human's "survivability quotient" on the basis of our ability to organize so as   not to be wiped out by very real cosmic hazards from comets, asteroids and the nuclear furnace we call the Sun.

What is the Purpose of Human Existence?

If we pass Arthur's first IQ test and find a way to produce   an effective human strategy to protect the world   against cosmic hazards, there is the next basic question of why are humans worth saving and what are we good for anyway?   It is an extreme egoism of the human race that we constantly self-congratulate ourselves on having achieved the top intelligence on our small planet. This seems a bit arrogant in that chimpanzees and bonobos share an incredibly high percentage of the DNA structure of humans. Recently the courts in the U.S. have heard a case as to whether chimpanzees can sue to gain their independence from slavery from human captors.

The most arrogant of the human race takes the basic premise of Rene Descartes and extends it further to say: "I think, therefore I am, and therefore I should be." Arthur C. Clarke, however, frequently suggested that human ingenuity, as an evolved capability, was not an entitlement but rather an opportunity to achieve a higher calling. In short, Clarke suggested, that humans were perhaps created only as part of a longer term cosmic destiny to ultimately build a greater intelligence with a higher moral ethos. He specifically suggested that the purpose of humans was not the capitalist dream of accumulating wealth or building estates, but rather to seek knowledge and create beauty.

Clarke suggested that artificial machine intelligence superior to human intelligence was only a matter of time because of the speed of artificial evolution in comparison to the slowness of biological evolution. In a whimsical perspective—so typical of his wry humor—he suggested that we must simply hope that our superior silicon friends will be kind to their dimwitted co-inhabitants of planet Earth that are destined to lag behind smart machines with superior heuristic algorithms that will inevitably arise during the 21st century. Ray Kurzweil, author of _The Singularity is Near_, has suggested that the point where artificial intelligence crosses over to exceed typical human intelligence is at hand. As noted earlier, Henry Markham's Blue Brain Project has projected that it will be able to approximate human brain functionality as of 2023. In light of the rapid and ongoing research it does seem likely that this crucial crossover will occur sometime soon. In terms of the vast span of cosmic time, it makes little difference as to whether crossover or the age of the singularity is achieved in 2023, 2033 or 2043—this new age is coming and human society is ill-prepared for this transition.

In any event Clarke suggested that this transition to a time when machines can "out-think us" will be a "good thing". In his mind this crossover will force humanity to contemplate the true meaning of human existence and if there is a purpose to life in the vast cosmos. And what "purpose" can be ascribed to human existence? One of Clarke's close intellectual collaborators, R. Buckminster Fuller, spoke of the human ability to engage in ephemeralization or truly home run, game changing innovation. To Fuller this might ultimately prove to be the entire meaning of life—the ability to create order in the universe. Whatever one calls life—and especially intelligent life—it ultimately results in new knowledge, in beauty, design, or order and structure. Within the natural universe we find positive and negative, heat and cold, light and dark, but according to the Second Law of Thermodynamics the universe only experiences the one way process of entropy. Entropy, according the physics of thermodynamics, is universally a one way process in all natural states to move consistently to a state that is more disordered and non-predictable. Such a universal process would suggest that the ultimate result for the cosmos must be total disorder with no structure. If this the case how can life, intelligent life, and knowledge and beauty be created? For Fuller the answer is that life—and particularly intelligent life—could become an "anti-entropic force" within the universe. Clarke does not come to the same conclusion, but he suggests that the fundamental purpose of humans is to create knowledge and beauty. This seems to be what he had in mind when he said: "It may be that our role on this planet is not to worship God but to create him."

If artificial intelligence evolves to the point so that its feedback loops allow for more and more innovation and improved rates of "intellectual efficiency" then this would seem to allow for order, coherent design, knowledge and beauty also to accelerate. We might find a way to create "anti- entropy" and restructure the second law of thermo-dynamics.

One might jump to the conclusion from this logic to suggest that humans are "ordained to succeed" in a quest to create new knowledge, beauty and anti-entropic structure in the universe. This would assume, however, that life exists only on Earth and that humans are the only highly advanced form of intelligence. Maybe other intelligences elsewhere in the universe might have already unlocked these secrets of the cosmos. Perhaps when we find the answer known as the Grand United Theory, or "GUTS" that explains the relationship between the four known forces in the universe, i.e. gravity, electro-magnetic forces, the weak nuclear force and the strong nuclear force we will be able to unlock this mystery also.

We now have sophisticated astronomical observatory telescope satellites such as Hubble, Chandra, Keppler and in a short while others such as the James Webb optical telescope that can probe the universe to find other star systems with planets. To date we have identified a thousand planets including some that could support the existence of water and life.

It is still an unsolved mystery as to whether there is life elsewhere and especially if there is intelligent life on other planets. We certainly do not know if it is the purpose of all life, including particularly intelligent life, to create knowledge, overcome entropy and restore order and coherence to the cosmos. The search for this answer began in serious intent in the middle of the 20th century and continues today.

The ever increasing effort to detect radio signals from other star systems has led to the building of new, very large array systems such as the one in New Mexico in the United States. This SETI (Search for Extra-Terrestrial Intelligence) process has been searching the skies since 1960 at the radio telescope in Greenback, West Virginia. But it was a major grant from Paul Allen to the SETI cause in 2013 that has given a recent boost to this increasingly serious effort.

In the meantime, Clarke's statement of human purpose as striving to add knowledge and beauty may well have to do. Currently at the societal level we humans put more value and emphasis on economic growth and creation of new wealth and physical assets than we do to survival of the species. Certainly intellectual advancement and creation of beauty might make the top ten list of human aspirations, but in a capitalist economy focused on growth it is far from number one. It is even far from clear whether modern human society will survive or whether we can evolve to a higher state.

Two quotes from Arthur about humans and the purpose of intelligent life put things in perspective. The first is the quite serious statement: "It has yet to be proven that intelligence has any survival value." And the second is the satirical, wry, yet thought provoking: "The best proof that there's intelligent life in outer space is the fact that it hasn't come here." Clarke in his thoughts about human purpose, inevitably comes back to the fundamental issue of whether human—or at least intelligent -- life are a unique occurrence in the vast universe. Is life and thinking creatures an inevitable outcome needed to restore balance to the physical universe to overcome entropy. As Clarke has said: "Two possibilities exist: Either we are alone in the Universe or we are not. Both are equally terrifying." Until we unlock this puzzle it will remain difficult, if not impossible, to say what the purpose of humanity actually is.

Intelligence versus Survival?

Humans are a substandard breed in many ways. Our birth and sexual processes are complicated and difficult. Other animals can run faster, live longer, climb more skillfully, fly without mechanical assistance, and are more resistant to disease. Some would argue that medical research, drugs, and prosthetics will in the longer term make humans more prone to debilitating disease. The one advantage that humans seem to have is a superior brain—a thousand time more capable than that of a rat. The evolution of the brain might have many possible purposes. The assumption that humans tend to make is that intelligence is for a purpose and many believe that this is linked to ultimate survival. The dinosaurs that were wiped out in the K-T mass extinction event 65 million years ago are often the butt of jokes about not being smart enough to survive a massive asteroid strike. But the dinosaur era lasted for about 167 million years (or from about 232 million years ago to about 65 million). In contrast, *homo sapiens* have to date only lasted about 200,000 years. In short, if we were to put human staying power up against the dinosaurs they lasted 835 times longer than people, as of 2015.

If we are to compare humans to insects or ferns on the survivability scale the insects and ferns would win by a vast margin. The haunting question that Clarke and many anthropologists have considered quite seriously is whether intelligence is the key to survival? And if so in what way is it important? Is intelligence key because of its ability to unlock means of escape? Is it essential for humans to eventually create enough technology for us to escape the Earth's gravity well and eventually to colonize other planets and escape one solar system before the Sun explodes and dies? Is intelligence important to be able to connect to other intelligences across the vast reaches of the cosmos in order to learn key knowledge or re-engineer the structure of the universe to make it survivable?

Clarke indeed sought to probe such issues by thinking of the vast reaches of space and re-engineering of planets at one level. But he also sought to probe the mysteries of such things as chaos theory, non-linear math, and the meaning of mathematics to seek theoretical answers as well. He often came back to the question of why we have not yet connected with intelligent life, if it is indeed out there. Clarke's answered this at several levels. First he responded to skeptics and fundamentalist religious figures as follows: "The fact that we have not yet found the slightest evidence for life — much less intelligence — beyond this Earth does not surprise or disappoint me in the least. Our technology must still be laughably primitive; we may well be like jungle savages listening for the throbbing of tom-toms, while the ether around them carries more words per second than they could utter in a lifetime." Others such as Carl Sagan sought to categorize human science and technology by a metric he devised based on the amount of power and energy at the command of humans and the amount of information to which they had access. His conclusion is that other civilizations that evolved well before humans would have access to much more energy and information and thus we need to become much more capable before we can actually connect.

Arthur C. Clarke's assessment that we are now evolving our scientific and engineering systems at an increasingly fast rate should allow us to achieve enormous breakthroughs in our capabilities. His estimate is that we should be able to accomplish much of what we can "conceive of" within the window of the next three hundred years. This would therefore seem to include the development of fusion-based reactors for travel to the stars, the ability to control the Earth's climate, to find a cure for all diseases, discover the way to control population growth so as to not destabilize natural balances or use up the world's resources, and to supply low-cost and plentiful green energy to all peoples of the world, and to engineer smart robots or cyborgs to carry out work as it was previously understood.

In such a world, we would need to rethink almost everything such as the meaning and purpose of "work", "territorial sovereignty", "war", "capitalism", "wealth" and even "poverty". In such a world of plenty would humans be able to escape from their heritage of dominance, criminal behavior and one-upmanship over others of different ethnicity, class, race, religion, language or culture? In a Delphi survey that explored possible changes in the future almost every conceivable social, technical or cultural innovation was thought possible at some time in the future—space travel, access to limitless electronic or nuclear power, even teleportation. The one change that was thought most unlikely to occur was in humans wearing clothes. This retention of clothing was directly linked to human attachment to status and feelings of dominance that comes from millions of years of atavistic tribalism. Everyone in the Delphi Survey thought that humans would hang on to status and class structure and thus their clothes—forever.

The predictions of Arthur C. Clarke were indeed remarkable and often amazingly on target. Yet his real lasting place in history will not be his predictions about communications satellites, space elevators, nuclear fusion, driverless cars, DNA testing or the Internet.. His true legacy will be in his aspirations for a human race with a higher purpose and its future evolution to a higher level of attainment. In his science fiction he addressed a human future that reflected a species that overcomes avarice, war, and aggression. He created visions of super high-rise living towers in the sky that reached a tenth of the way to the Moon and left the floor of Planet Earth to sustain the richness of natural flora and fauna. He foresaw humanity traveling to the stars, creating super artificial intelligence of incredible mental capacity, and in *Childhood's End* he even envisions all human's linking their mind's together in a universal brain-meld that led to a new evolutionary step forward into the unknown.

If we were to create an Institute of the Future devoted to Arthur C. Clarke's inspiration for evolved humanity its manifest for research might include the following goals:

a. Limitless green and recyclable energy and advanced transportation and communications systems.

b. Ocean processing to provide potable, desalinated water, needed natural resources, as well as pollution removal and clean energy.

c. Plentiful, healthy, and recyclable food supply.

d. Technical, economic and social systems to allow normalization of global population sufficient to maintain genetic diviersity but not exceed the Earth's natural resources.

e. New economic and political systems that advance human survival and intellectual development rather than production throughput and aggression.

f. Atmospheric and water purification systems plus weather and natural disaster control capabilities.

g. Super human artificial intelligence systems to create the new technology for humans to survive on a cosmic time scale.

h. Cure to all known disease and perhaps genetic design of off springs.

i. Heat and energy transfer systems to outer space to rebalance the Earth's thermal overload and to normalize the climate.

j. Cosmic hazard systems to deflect asteroids and comets from Earth impact.

k. Magnetic protection shield systems for Planet Earth to divert solar storms that could destroy vital modern infrastructure.

l. Space elevators for transport and cosmic heat pipes.

m. Interstellar travel capability so that humanity could outlive the sun. (Perhaps this might include either anti-gravity systems or even time travel.)

n. Creative new efforts to find intelligent extraterrestrial life in the universe.

o. Ethnic, racial, cultural, social and economic harmony for humanity.

Today, in the U.S., the National Academies of Science and Engineering have 'grand challenge' research objectives that focus on some of what might be called the"early end" of Clarke's hypothetical list of advanced capabilities and aspirations that might have achieved for the future. Before the end of the 21st century, however, scientists and engineers will need to think on a much grander scale than ever before. Cosmic defense systems against asteroids or against severe solar storms might require building space systems with structural areas larger than that of the Earth's surface. Cosmic heat pipes and magnetic force fields might need to be tens of thousands of kilometers in length. In a future world where such cosmic space projects might be needed to defend Earth, we humans might finally begin to think beyond petty wars over national boundaries and jihads against those with offending religious beliefs.

Arthur often quoted science fiction writer Larry Niven who famously said: "The dinosaurs did not survive because they did not have a good space program." Yet we have not only put off ending wars and religious strife, we have yet to implement seriously Clarke's Project Safeguard that would defend us from cosmic hazards. When we look to humanity's current track record of fighting wars, engaging in religious and ethnic strife, and our inability to cope effectively with climate change and cosmic hazards, such as potentially hazardous asteroids and coronal mass ejections, it is sometimes hard to be optimistic about the future.

Yet one of the great things about Sir Arthur is that he always believed humanity to be better than we currently are. Yet he—and I—have great hope and continued optimistic aspirations for the future. The answer, as discussed in the first chapter, are just emphasizing the good three I's and de-emphasizing the bad three I's. Again, that 6 I's formula is simply that we need to evolve as a race to be more Intelligent, more Innovative, more Imaginative and not be quite so Ignorant, Insensitive and Immoral.

Arthur's creative and humanistic philosophy will remain relevant even many centuries from now. We should pay particular heed to the following profound Clarke-ism: "As our own species is in the process of proving, one cannot have superior science and inferior morals. The combination is unstable and self-destroying."

We should particularly pay attention to the reason that Arthur felt space travel was so important to humanity when he said: "It is not easy to see how the more extreme forms of nationalism can long survive when men have seen the Earth in its true perspective as a single small globe against the stars." He could easily have said the same about extreme forms of religion that now pits one form of prescribed religious practice against another, He strongly felt that as humans evolve and travel out to the stars that we must strive for a common high moral standard of justice, trust, compassion and ethical sustainability. Arthur, in essence, saw the universe as an ethical continuum that could be revealed by mathematics, science, and intellectual pursuit. These efforts by humans—and in time "our gifted companion thinking algorithms"—can eventually unlock the philosophical integrity of a cosmos with a consistency and logic that could become the true universal religion. The universal judge that some call natural selection and some call the "almighty", might in time serve to unite all thinking beings wherever they might exist across the cosmos.

Until that heroic accomplishment is achieved the questions and moral imperatives of Sir Arthur Clarke will indeed remain relevant and pertinent to our lives.

Technology or Application	Predictions	Today's Reality or Future Trend
APPENDIX 1 **Arthur C. Clarke Predictions Compared to Today's Technology and Systems**		
Bio-Engineering and Artificial Intelligence		
Bio-engineering as well as Birth Control Pill and DNA Testing.	Many concepts of this nature were in *Childhood's End* (1953). Specific ideas about Cyborgs came later. Arthur C. Clarke's protagonist in the novella *A Meeting with Medusa* (1971). Cyborgs can be accomplished by either artificial evolution of other life forms or embedded chips and mechanical parts added to humans. Other sci-fi writers also wrote on these topics at a later date such as Ursula Le Guin, Phillip Farmer, etc.. Such ideas as well as mutant slaves were also envisioned in the movie *Total Recall that was based on the Philip K. Dick short story "We Can Remember It for You Wholesale."*	Embedding chips for a variety of applications. Artificial organs, muscles, and limbs. We are on the verge of the capability to grow cloned replacement of human organs. Henry Markham and Ray Kurzweil have talked of creating an artificial brain that is equivalent to 10^{17} of memory and 10^{18} flops of computer processing power. Human brain is limited to 100 trillion synapses, but this could be augmented in the cloud with petabytes of exabytes of digital synapses.

Artificial Intelligence and Expert Systems	"Artificial Intelligence is the most important technological development of the 20th Century" - Arthur C. Clarke, Comsat Corporation 1976.	"AI" and "expert systems" are today replacing humans in such jobs such as property assessors, pharmacists, commercial artists and designers, bank tellers, etc. Prof. Markham claims to be able to soon simulate a human brain.
Mechanical Evolution of "Smart" Robots Exceeding Human Intelligence	HAL in 2001:A Space Odyssey (1968). Note: HAL stood for **H**euristic **A**lgorithm and not IBM spelt one letter backwards. Let's hope our silicon successors will be kind to humans. Predictions beyond Artificial Intelligence-the use of Von Neumann machines to transform Jupiter into a minmor star system (Concept in the book 2010)	Robots for industrial, police and household tasks now available. Ray Kurzweil - *"The Singularity is Near"* - within 20 years smart robots will be able to start replacing a majority of service industry workforce. Some, including Arthur C. Clarke, think that "machines" and software driven evolution will soon outstrip biological evolution. As noted above, crossover point is projected to be 2023.

Space Related Concepts, Applications or Technologies		
Geo Synchronous Space Communication Systems	Predicted or "envisioned" in 1945 in *Extraterrestrial Relays* and *Space Stations* both in <u>*Wireless World.*</u> In his <u>*Islands in the Sun*</u> in 1952 Arthur C. Clarke not only described a communications satellite but also described antennas to support inter-regional intersatellite links between Geo satellites.	Realized in 1963/64 by Hughes Syncom satellite launched by NASA. Early Bird operational in 1965. Japanese OICETs and European Artemis conducted optimal intersatellite links. RF intersatellite links between LEO satellites carried out on Iridium satellites from 1998. Today over 300 Geo satellites in operation supporting over $100 billion/ year (US) in revenues and sales.
Cell Phones-Satellite Phones	BBC show of 1964. Envisioned in both science and Sci-Fi books by Arthur C. Clarke. He recalled even earlier predictions of today's capabilities that were made in 19th century. In Aug. 1956 in a letter to Andrew Haley he wrote: "It might make possible world-wide person-to-person radio with automatic dialing. Thus no one on the planet ever need be out of touch with the community, unless he wanted to be."	Access to broadband smart cell phones today anywhere and at any time. Satellite phones available on airplanes, ships, etc., via Iridium, Globalstar, Inmarsat, and Thuraya, Terrestar, etc. 4G LTE cell phones with ubiquitous low cost broadband mobile communications in most urban/suburban locations. With the new DVB-SH standard TV television service to satellite phone from mobile satellites with 22 meter deployable antennas in Geo orbit.

Satellite Television	Envisioned by Arthur C. Clarke in both science and Sci-Fi books. This was a prominent aspect of his 1945 article.	Satellite video and global interconnectivity. First satellite relay was via Telstar and Relay in 1962. Today television available globally via 20,000 satellite television channels. Soon Satellite TV to handheld units.
Satellites for Space Navigation	Use of satellites for navigation and position determination. This was indicated as an application accessible by a wristwatch like device in his 1945 article. Noted it would likely involve orbits lower than Geo.	GPS - Navstar system of US. Also in USSR/ Russia GLONASS system (since 1970s). These space navigation and positioning systems are now joined by systems of China, India, Europe and Japan.
Extensive Global Networks. INTERNET WWW, E-Commerce & Wikipedia	Time article in 1965 that predicted global computer networking, e-tail services and on-line encyclopedia. Networks that provides information to the world in real time without censorship will prevent atrocities and even governmental crimes against humanities (1972)-- *Report from Planet Three and Other Speculations*	Capabilities have increasingly come into being since the late 1980s.
Computer Networking Problems and Millennium Bug	*The Ghost From The Grand Banks* (1990) This was perhaps one of the first times this issue was explicit raise.	A number of issues are now being address from Millennium Bug to Leap Second adjustment problems for GPS time stamping.

Space Transportation	Mass Drivers on the Lunar Surface, *Journal of the British Interplanetary Society* (1950). Dr. Gerard O'Neill of Princeton University in *The High Frontier* further developed these ideas in his books about space colonies and colonies on the Moon. Also predicted gravitation slingshot maneuvers used in Rendezvous with Rama and other stories including in *2001: A Space Odyssey.* Nuclear Fusion Drive space ships. *Used in Songs of Distant Earth* (1952)	High speed maglev trains now in development and actual use. This has been the subject of a NASA study to build an multi-kilometer high mountain for mass driver launch from Earth. Ideas still being pursued but not yet realized. Gravitation slingshot assist used on Voyager 1 (1975) and with Ulysses solar research mission. Short burst fusion power with heavy hydrogen now achieved on Earth.
Project Safeguard	Rendezvous with Rama A project to detect threats to Earth from Near Earth Objects, Comets and Meteorites. Often quoted Larry Niven's remark that: The reason the dinosaurs are extinct is because they did not have a space program..	NASA has initiated this under U.S. Government funding. It is behind schedule. Project Sentinel, if launched would provide 100 year warning system for asteroids down to 30 meter to 40 meter in diameter.

Low Earth and Polar Earth Orbits for new applications	Use of low and polar orbiting systems for remote sensing, meteorology, communications and surveillance.	Today: Iridium, Globalstar and Orbcomm for communications. Polar orbit satellites for remote sensing, and meteorological applications. Aurora and other systems for spy satellites /surveillance.
Medical and Educational Services		
Tele-education and Tele-medicine	BBC Show of 1964 predicting wide spread usage of tele-education and tele-medicine in the future.. Clarke speech at UNESCO in 1978 in favor of using satellites for these purposes. Indicated that low cost devices for tele-education and tele-encyclopedias might have as much to do with the toy maker Matell as with IBM and personal computers.	Over 10 million students receiving tele-education in China. Millions more in India, Indonesia, and Mexico as well as in highly developed countries. Michael DeBekey performed surgery in Switzerland and explained his technique to doctors via the Intelsat 1 satellite (Early Bird) in 1965. NASA and research into Space Surgery: see Dr. Marlene Grenon of the Univ. of California San Francisco.
Accelerated and Sub conscious Education	Concept of new forms of education achieved by down loading of new knowledge while asleep. Learn another language while in suspended animation. Other astronauts on ship in _2001: A Space Odyssey_	Experiments with hypnosis and sleep based learning have not been successful. Connection of brain to embedded chips may well be much more successful. In short this prediction not yet realized.

Suspended Animation for Subsequent Medical Treatment	Freezing people with untreatable medical ailments. Could be thawed out and cured at a future time. This could be one way to address medical problems for which we now have no cure. Suspended Animation for People: The Journey to Jupiter and its satellites in *2001: A Space Odyssey*. It was also used in the short story *Songs of Distant Earth* (1956) that also became a novel 30 years later.	Failed experiments to date. Current freezing programs found to be medically fraudulent. Serious research, however, is now underway.
Broadband Communications and Transportation		
E-Mail	"Everybody in Instant Touch" - *The Coming of the Space Age (1967)*. Electronic communications can and probably will replace conventional mail. "Technology and the Future" Report on Planet Three (1972).	The volume of e-mail exchange is now measured in petabytes with over 1 billion on Facebook. This would now represent the third largest country, only behind China and India.
Tele-commuting	BBC Show of 1964 - predicted the widespread growth of telecommuting,	Millions now telecommute - people in Korea, India, Pakistan , Russia work as computer programmers for clients in U.S. and Europe. IBM, HP and other high tech companies each have 50,000+ telecommuters. See "Electronic Immigrants" - J.Pelton *Futurist* magazine 1967.

Automated cars	"Technology and the Future" _Report on Planet Three_. (1972)	The Google driverless car has now driven thousands of miles on California highways and roads as of 2014. Other systems under development in Japan and elsewhere.
Communications eliminating the need for Hub-Cities.	Clarke predicted creation of smart telecities, exo-cities, suburbs, exo-urbs with broadband communications -. BBC interview (1965). In time no need to live where one works. Living in a "tele-city" where easy communications and transport instantaneously available; e.g. in the "Space elevator cities" with tens of thousands of floors in the sky; Earth is transformed into a game park.	There are plans for telecities. Teletopia in Japan. Satellite cities and metacities advocated by many. Electronic Immigrants now in excess of 1 million. (i.e. people who live in one country and work in another.) (Future Talk, 1986) This could the first phase of "mind meld", i.e. _Childhood's End._
Energy Concepts and Technologies		
Ocean Thermal Energy Conversion	Arthur C. Clarke: "OTEC is the answer to OPEC" - in a lecture in Sri Lanka (1986)	Several projects under way today including Mitsubishi's OTEC plant to create liquid hydrogen off the Big Island in Hawaii.

Low Energy Nuclear Reactions (LENR) or Chemically Assisted Nuclear Reaction	Clarke: "There is something to this concept known perhaps incorrectly as 'cold fusion' that deserves serious study. It could revolutionize the world and provide us with boundless clean energy" (*Profiles of the Future*) Today the focus is on compact fusion by Lockheed Martin. Clarke clearly flagged "fusion" as key to our energy needs.	Serious study by hundreds of legitimate scientists, including physicist Luis Alvarez indicate that LENR can produce clean energy. "Cold fusion" in its new incarnation as low energy nuclear reaction may still prove to be a viable energy concept **still to be proven as is the concept of compact fusion**
Creating Stars from Giant Gaseous Planets	Power to sustain space colonies from reinvented stars. This was the surprise ending of *2010*.	We are still trying to create viable nuclear fusion reactors. When we do we may indeed ultimately be able to morph Jupiter into a new energy source. **Another prediction still to be realized.**
Space Travel and Living in Space		
Commercial Space Tourism and Transport	Arthur Clarke spoke in the late 1980s of the potential of "citizen astronauts" going into space on commercial spaceplanes	Commercial space planes carrying civilians on suborbital flights are to begin in 2015-2016. Hypersonic destination flights are projected for the 2020s or 2030s.
Space Elevator	Concept outlined in detail in *Fountain of Paradise* (1979)	NASA incentive prizes for solar powered robot climbers and nanotube fibers for 100,000 kilometer long cables. Space Elevator Corp. **Another prediction still to be realized.**

Terra forming of Planets	Clarke used this theme in several sci-fi stories with the first instance being Sands of Mars (1951). Objective of creating a sustainable lunar or planetary base. He even envisioned creating a star to sustain an ice-bound Europa (Satellite of Jupiter) to be able to sustain life. Term invented by Jack Williamson in 1942.	Elon Musk of Space X has the objective of terra-forming Mars as a stated long term goal for his company. Gerard O Neill envisioned how we could create an artificial planet at LaGrange points. **Another prediction still to be realized.**
Replicators	Ability to transport not people, plants and animals but "DNA" instructions to build "things" and "life forms" in distant locations. We could send "replicators" into space. *Profiles of the Future, 1962*.	3D printers in common use by 3D Printing, Hewlett Packard and EXAONE. Prof. Freeman Dyson of Princeton has described the potential of "Genome Eggs". If we understood the language of genomes we could send "genome eggs" to other planet that could grow habitats or new life forms. **This is another prediction still to be accomplished.**

APPENDIX 2

Summary List of Arthur C. Clarke Predictions Now Achieved

(Dates of prediction are provided in parentheses)

1. AUTOMATED CARS (1972)
2. BIRTH CONTROL PILL (1953)
3. BROADCASTING SATELLITES (1945)
4. ROBOTS WITH INTELLIGENCE (1968)
5. DNA TESTING (1953)
6. E-COMMERCE (1965)
7. FACSIMILE MACHINE (1953)
8. GLOBAL WIRELESS COMMUNICATIONS AND MOBILE PHONES (1956/1964)
9. GRAVITY ASSIST MANEUVERS TO INCREASE VELOCITY OF SPACECRAFT (1968)
10. INTERNET, WORLD WIDE WEB, GLOBAL NETWORKING (1962-1965)
11. INTERSATELLITE LINKS (1952)
12. ION DRIVE PROPULSION FOR SPACECRAFT (1968)
13. MAN ON THE MOON-MOON LANDING (1953)
14. MILLENNIUM BUG AS A POTENTIAL PROBLEM (1990)
15. NAVIGATION SATELLITES (1945)
16. NOTEPAD COMPUTERS (1968)
17. SAFEGUARD PROGRAM TO PROTECT AGAINST ASTEROIDS (1972)
18. SATELLITES FOR SEARCH AND RESCUE (1945)
19. SATELLITES FOR COMMUNICATIONS AND NAVIGATION FOR AIRCRAFT (1945)
20. "SMART" SUPER COMPUTERS (1968)
21. TELECOMMUNICATIONS SATELLITES (1945)
22. TELE-COMMUTING (1964)
23. TELE-EDUCATION (1964)
24. TELE-HEALTH--TELE-MEDICINE (1964)
25. VIDEO PHONES (1968)

APPENDIX 3

Summary List of Arthur C. Clarke Predictions
Yet to Be Realized

(Dates of prediction are provided in parentheses)

1. ANTI-GRAVITY—POSITRONIC DRIVE SYSTEMS (1953 onward)

2. CLIMATE CONTROL (1999)

3. CONTACT WITH EXTRA-TERRESTRIAL INTELLIGENCE (1953)

4. LARGE SCALE MINING OF THE SEA (1962)

5. MANNED MARS LANDING (1953)

6. MATTER TRANSMITTER (1953)

7. NUCLEAR FUSION (ON A CONTROLLED BASIS) (1962)

8. SPACE ELEVATORS (1962)

9. SPACE COLONIES (1953)

10. STAR SHIPS (1953)

11. TERRAFORMING OF PLANETS (1951)

APPENDIX 4

COMPANIES, ORGANIZATIONS AND GOVERNMENTAL ENTITIES THAT HAVE IMPLEMENTED TECHNOLOGY PREDICTED BY ARTHUR C. CLARKE

AUTOMATED "DRIVERLESS" CARS	1972	Google
BIRTH CONTROL PILL	1953	Johnson and Johnson, Pfizer, etc.
BROADCASTING SATELLITES	1945	GE, SES of Luxembourg, DirecTV, DISH-Echostar
DNA TESTING	1953	Police Forces, Prosecutors and Court Systems around the world, DNA labs
E-COMMERCE	1965	Google, Amazon, Ali Baba, E-Bay
FACSIMILE MACHINE	1953	Hewlett Packard, Panasonic, etc.
GLOBAL WIRELESS COMMUNICATIONS AND MOBILE PHONES	1956-1964	AT&T, Verizon, T-Mobile, British Telecom, Samsung, Motorola, Vodafone, etc.
GRAVITY ASSIST MANEUVERS TO INCREASE VELOCITY OF SPACECRAFT	1968	NASA, ESA, Lockheed Martin, etc.
INTERNET, WORLD WIDE WEB, GLOBAL NETWORKING	1962-65	Google, AOL, Microsoft, etc.
INTERSATELLITE LINKS	1952	Motorola, Lockheed Martin, Boeing
ION DRIVE PROPULSION FOR SPACECRAFT	1968	Boeing, L-3 ETI, Lockheed Martin, HyperV Technology Corp.,
MANNED LUNAR MISSION	1953	TRW, Northrop Grumman

MILLENNIUM BUG AS A POTENTIAL PROBLEM	1990	National Governments
NAVIGATION SATELLITES	1945	Lockheed Martin, Boeing
NOTEPAD COMPUTERS	1968	Apple, Samsung, Acer, etc.
SAFEGUARD PROGRAM TO PROTECT AGAINST ASTEROIDS	1972	Planetary Society, B612 Foundation, NASA, ESA, etc.
SATELLITES FOR COMMUNICATIONS AND NAVIGATION FOR AIRCRAFT	1945	Air Bus, Lockheed Martin, Boeing, ARINC, INMARSAT, etc.
"SMART" and "VERBAL" SUPER COMPUTERS	1969	IBM WATSON, CRAY, Fujitsu, Intel, Nor-Tech, etc.
TELECOMMUNICATIONS SATELLITES	1945	Thales Alenia, Boeing, Lockheed Martin, Air Bus
TELE-COMMUTING	1964	Hewlett Packard, AT&T, Jet Blue, etc.
TELE-EDUCATION	1964	Jones International University, UK Open University
TELE-HEALTH-TELE-MEDICINE	1964	AMD Global Telemedicine, Ameridoc, InTouch Health, etc.
VIDEO PHONE COMMUNICATION	1968	Skype, Webex, Go to Meeting

BIOGRAPHIES

About the Author

Joseph N. Pelton, author of the *Oracle of Colombo,* is the award winning author or editor of some 40 books and over 300 articles in the field of space, satellite communications systems, and technology. His books include *Global Talk,* which was nominated for a Pulitzer Prize, *Basics of Satellite Communications, Handbook of Cosmic Hazards and Planetary Defense, Handbook of Satellite Applications, e-Sphere: The Rise of the World Wide Mind, MegaCrunch,* and *Future Shock.* In July 2013 he received in the UK the International Award known as "The Arthurs" in honor of Arthur C. Clarke. He also received the Arthur C. Clarke Foundation's Lifetime Achievement award in 2001. He played a key role in the founding of the Arthur C. Clarke Foundation which he announced at the White House in 1983 while he acted as Managing Director of the World Communications Year panel—a US Presidential Appointment. Dr. Pelton is also known as a futurist and is a member of the International Advisory Board of the World Future Society.

He is the Director Emeritus of the Space and Advanced Communications Research Institute (SACRI) at George Washington University where he headed various programs for nearly a decade. He served as Chairman of the Board (1992-95) and Vice President of Academic Programs and Dean (1995-96) of the International Space University in Strasbourg, France. From 1988 to 1996 Dr. Pelton was Director of the Interdisciplinary Telecommunications Program at the University of Colorado Boulder. Dr. Pelton also held a number of executive positions at the COMSAT Corporation and at INTELSAT where among other duties he headed strategic planning and Project SHARE. He has carried out projects for NASA, NTIA, the U.S. Congress, the United Nations, AT&T, the International Engineering Consortium, Orbital Sciences, the Korean and

Indonesian Governments, the Satellite Industry Association, Telecom Italia, and many others.

Dr. Pelton is a Fellow of the International Association for the Advancement of Space Safety (IAASS) and a member of its Executive Board and Chairman of its Academic Committee. He is also the former President of the International Space Safety Foundation. He was the founding president of the Society of Satellite Professionals International and the Global Legal Information Network (GLIN). Dr. Pelton was elected to full membership in the International Academy of Astronautics in 1998 and was elected to the Hall of Fame of the Society of Satellite Professionals International in 2001, an honor extended to less than 100 people in the field. In 2004 he was elected an Associate Fellow of the American Institute of Aeronautics and Astronautics.   Dr. Pelton is a frequent speaker around the world; he has delivered talks in over twenty countries, at the UN and appeared on media, including the BBC, FR3, ABC, NBC, and National Public Radio.

Joseph N. Pelton received his Ph.D. from Georgetown University, his Masters from New York University and his BS from the University of Tulsa. He lives in Arlington, Virginia.

About the Editor

Peter Marshall began as a journalist with BBC radio and television news, later becoming a News Editor. In 1966, he moved to Visnews of London (then part-owned by the BBC, and now Reuters-TV), a global TV news agency where he became General Manager. He was a pioneer in the use of satellites for TV news coverage and distribution and in 1986, he moved to Washington DC to create the Broadcast Services Division of the inter-governmental body INTELSAT. With the emergence of deregulation and competition, he returned to the private sector as President of Keystone

Communications, a satellite services provider serving international TV markets. This organization, is now part of Globecast (a subsidiary of France Telecom) which is the largest provider of global satellite broadcast services.

Peter Marshall is a past Chairman of the Royal Television Society in the UK, past President of the Society of Satellite Professionals (SSPI) in the USA and he was elected to the SSPI's "Hall of Fame" in 2006 in recognition of his pioneering work for the industry. He continues to serve as a member of the Board of the Arthur C. Clarke Foundation.

He is now a writer and consultant, based in his native U.K., and he has collaborated with Dr. Pelton on seven books and major research projects, including *Communications Satellites – Global Change Agents* (published by Lawrence Erlbaum in 2006), *Space Exploration and Astronaut Safety* (AIAA , 2007) , *License to Orbit – the Future of Commercial Space Travel* (Apogee Books, 2011) and *Launching Into Commercial Space* (AIAA 2013).

---------------0------------0------------0---------------

THE
ARTHUR C. CLARKE
FOUNDATION

The Arthur C. Clarke Foundation was established in 1983 in Washington, D.C., as part of the World Communications Year celebrations.The Foundation was created to recognize and promote the extraordinary contributions of Arthur C. Clarke to the world, to promote the use of space and telecommunications technology for the benefit of humankind, and to promote education and training in the fields of science, technology, engineering, the arts, and math (STEAM).

The Foundation has made scholarship awards, hosted space related symposia, championed the cause of space safety, assisted with museum exhibits, given awards to exceptional people, and worked for many years in cooperation with sister organizations such as the Arthur C. Clarke Institute for Space Education, the Arthur C. Clarke Center for the Human Imagination at the University of California-San Diego, the International Space University, the International Association for the Advancement of Space Safety, the Challenger Center, the Children's Space Shuttle Foundation, the Japan-US Science, Technology and Space Applications Program (JUSTSAP), the Universities Space Research Association, and the British Interplanetary Society. Official book projects of the Foundation include: Neil McAleer's *Visionary, Space 30* and now this current book *The Oracle of Colombo: How Arthur C. Clarke Revealed the Future.*

The Clarke Foundation provides support to: (i) the Clarke Award for the outstanding Challenger Center classroom; (ii) The John L. McLucas Space Safety Fund; (iii) the International Association for the Advancement of Space Safety (IAASS) and the *Journal of Space Safety Engineering;* (iv) the International Space University (ISU); (v) the National Electronics Museum space exhibit; (vi) the Burton I. Edelson Scholarship at George Washington University; (vii) the Huish School Outstanding Student of the Year Award; the British Interplanetary Society; (viii) the Global Space Institute; (ix) the World Future Society; and (x) the Global Space Governance study at McGill University of Montreal, Canada.

The author, as Managing Director for the U.S. Committee for World Communications Year, is proud to have recruited the first Board of Directors for the Arthur C. Clarke Foundation and served as its first Managing Director, along with Dr. John McLucas, its first Chairman of its Board, Fred C. Durant, its Executive Director, and Tedson C. Meyers, its first legal counsel.

42615572R00125

Made in the USA
Charleston, SC
03 June 2015